DISCOVER THE WISDOM OF MICHAEL FOR
YOURSELF....

- How love can eliminate fear and regain
  paradise
- How to be a golden star of light
- How to recognize the angels that hover
  protectively around you at all times
- What the fragrance of roses can tell you
- Why the color pink has extraordinary
  significance
- How to recognize a celestial bridge upon
  the path of your lifestream
- How to use a meditative exercise to create
  a sacred space
- Where to find places of great spiritual
  vibration upon the planet
- How to join the dance of love and light

And more affirmations, inspirations, and
divine truths

THE WISDOM TEACHINGS OF
ARCHANGEL MICHAEL

THE WISDOM TEACHINGS

of

ARCHANGEL MICHAEL

Through Lori Jean Flory
as told to Brad Steiger

A SIGNET VISIONS BOOK

SIGNET
Published by the Penguin Group
Penguin Books USA Inc., 375 Hudson Street,
New York, New York 10014, U.S.A.
Penguin Books Ltd, 27 Wrights Lane,
London W8 5TZ, England
Penguin Books Australia Ltd, Ringwood,
Victoria, Australia
Penguin Books Canada Ltd, 10 Alcorn Avenue,
Toronto, Ontario, Canada M4V 3B2
Penguin Books (N.Z.) Ltd, 182–190 Wairau Road,
Auckland 10, New Zealand

Penguin Books Ltd, Registered Offices:
Harmondsworth, Middlesex, England

First published by Signet, an imprint of Dutton Signet,
a division of Penguin Books USA Inc.

First Printing, January, 1997
10 9 8 7 6 5 4 3 2 1

REGISTERED TRADEMARK—MARCA REGISTRADA

Printed in the United States of America

Dedicated to my Angels of Light: my mom and dad, brothers, sister, and to my husband—my lifemate and soulmate. You are all gifts of love in my life that the Angels have blessed me with. I am grateful.

I would like to thank the following beautiful earth angels who have shared their guiding light, love, and support with me, blessing my heart so richly with their presence and their joy. First, I give gratitude and loving thanks to God, to Archangel Michael and to all of God's angels. I am also grateful to my mom and dad, two brothers, and my sister for blessing me with their beauty, love and presence. I am eternally grateful to my husband, Charles Flory, for his sense of humor, a bit of protection and unconditional love and support.

I am so very grateful to Brad Steiger and Sherry Hansen Steiger for their love, their friendship, faith and belief in Archangel Michael's messages of joy and their light-filled assistance—you have been a lighthouse shining your beam out over the waters of my life. Thank you to literary agent Agnes Birnbaum in helping Archangel Michael's book to be manifested—you are all beautiful blessings and your light enriches me!

To Dutton Signet and to our editor, Danielle Perez, our love and gratitude goes beyond words. Danielle, you are the very best!!! Thank you also from my heart, John Harricharan for your friendship, love, and support—you always believed in this project and never gave up on me! Thank you also, Lois East, Nancy Candler, Chris Williamson, Yolanda Martinez, Bernard Vardy, and Sean McCollar for your friendship, love, and support. I treasure each of you with heartfelt appreciation and light!

—Lori Jean Flory

Contents

CONTENTS

Contents

Contents

CHAPTER TEN: *We Are All Beings of Light 186*

CHAPTER ELEVEN: *The God Force Sustains Us All 203*

Contents

Introduction

October 27, 1993 began no differently from any other morning for Lori Jean and Charles Flory.

Lori Jean had got up at 4:30 A.M. to prepare Charles's breakfast and to make his lunch.

She fed their pets, kissed her husband good-bye, and was back in bed by about 5:30.

She was lying in bed, saying her I AM affirmations and praying, when she heard a loud, booming male voice say, "I want you!"

"I wasn't sleeping," Lori Jean insists. "I was meditative, relaxed, just lying there doing my affirmations. I heard the voice audibly. It was not in my head."

Lori Jean has been touched by the angels since she was a child of three. About the time she turned twenty-one, she established a regular process of communication with Daephrenocles, her angelic guide.

"I didn't feel it was Daephrenocles this time," she said. "The voice, the energy was different. While it was loving, it was powerful, almost overwhelming."

Lori Jean continued with her affirmations—until the voice once again interrupted her concentration: *"Lori Jean, let me speak to you. Let me tell you all about it."*

"Tell me all about what?" Lori Jean wondered—then kept meditating. She had been mentally asking for help with a health issue. She wanted to know if she would be okay.

She was relieved when she heard the same voice answer, yes, that she would be all right.

According to Lori Jean, Daephrenocles and other angelic beings frequently come to her and prompt her to go to her computer to transcribe the words that they dictate.

"I go into meditation at the computer, with my eyes closed, and the angels begin to type through my fingers," she explained. "I never know from one session to the next what they are going to write. I just let go, and they bring it through. I just pray that I always bring it through as they want it to be. When I meditate, I receive inner images, feelings, pictures, visions, and words."

In 1989 an angelic being claiming to be the Archangel Michael had manifested and told her that he would be working with her one day. On that occasion, the angel had appeared in their bedroom doorway, holding a globe in his hands.

"He was pure light," Lori Jean recalled, "so bright that I almost couldn't look at him."

And now she wondered if the angelic being who had summoned her that October morning in 1993 was Michael, wishing her to begin to receive messages at the keyboard of the computer.

"Yes!" the voice replied in response to her unspoken question.

Lori Jean became flustered. Why would such a mighty being as Archangel Michael come to her?

She did not go near the computer.

But the powerful energy lingered near her and followed her wherever she went.

She suddenly saw the image of a tall being with dark brown hair, blue eyes, a beard, and a mustache.

"Angels can appear however they choose," Lori Jean acknowledged, "but I believed the being to be Archangel Michael."

Lori Jean called her friend Lois East, an accomplished artist who is also a well-known deep trance psychic sensitive, and told her what was happening to her that morning.

"Lois said that she got big chills all over that it really was the Archangel Michael summoning me," Lori Jean said. "Chills are affirmations of truth. The angels just lovingly touch the edge of your soul's aura to give you a little chill of recognition."

With Lois's words of encouragement to bolster her fragile ego, Lori Jean finally sat down at the computer.

"To my complete astonishment, Michael told me that he would like to bring a book of wisdom teachings through me," Lori Jean said. "I thought again about his telling me something similar a few years before, about his wanting to work through me."

Although Lori Jean was honored by such words of attunement issuing forth from Archangel Michael, she still felt somewhat intimidated and reluctant to acknowledge that she might be worthy of such collaboration. "I am just an instrument. The light shines through me, but I am not the light. I work in partnership with the light and with the angels."

However, on November 5, 1993, Lois East did a reading that once again confirmed that Charles as well as Lori Jean had been chosen to bring forth Archangel Michael's book into the world.

On that same day, Charles and she were almost in an automobile accident.

"A lady pulled out in front of us just as we entered

a crossroads at a residential intersection near our house," Lori Jean recalled. "It was truly as if she had not seen us.

"I steered hard to the left, and we missed her by about two feet. I felt someone else take the wheel. Charles said that he could not stop staring at the steering wheel while this was occurring. I felt strangely calm through the whole episode.

"Later, Daephrenocles told us that a bubble of white light was put around us and that time was slowed down. He explained that a kind of molecular shift had taken place with our car in order to prevent us from being hit and being injured."

Reluctantly, but sincerely and with dedication, by November 8, Lori Jean had begun receiving dictation from Michael for the book that was to be manifested through her fingers working at the computer.

"After I had worked for a while bringing more information through for the book, I called Lois and asked why the angels had chosen me for this assignment," Lori Jean recalled.

"Why me, instead of some famous, nationally known person with the right connections who would really be able to do something with the book?"

She had no sooner uttered her insecurities when Lori Jean had a vision with her wide-open physical eyes of a large white hand suddenly breaking through the ceiling and pointing a finger directly at her.

"When I told Lois about the vision, she said that it was like a picture of Uncle Sam on a recruiting poster, saying, 'I want you!' Although the image was there for only a few seconds, I agreed with Lois that I guessed the vision had effectively answered my questions."

But as human nature would have it, that very next day, Lori Jean did not find time to sit down at the computer and make herself available to receive Michael's messages.

"About 8:30 P.M. as I was working in my office typing a fax to our friend John Harricharan before his departure to Australia, the lights went on and off," Lori Jean said. "I called to Charles in the living room, and he said there had been no disturbance with the lights.

"I thought this was strange—stranger still that my office lights had blinked on and off and not affected my computer.

"Suddenly I felt that this was Michael's way of reminding me of the importance of spending time each day working on the book.

"The lights went off and back on again, and I saw in the office before me a very tall being of light. The entity was all white light with a white robe of light.

Michael had said that I would become more aware of his presence as the project progressed.

" 'I'm sorry, Michael,' I said. 'I'll do better from now on.' "

A HUMBLE MESSENGER OF LIGHT

"I don't think this would work for me if I just sat at the computer and waited for information to come through," Lori Jean told me in February 1995. "It's after I have been meditating for a few minutes that the messages just start flowing through."

Michael Turns Off TV When It Is Time for Lori Jean to Receive

On occasion, she told me with a delightful girlish giggle, if she and Charles are spending a bit too long relaxing with an evening of television, Michael will simply turn off the set.

The first time that such an unscheduled interruption occurred during their regular evening programming, Lori Jean asked Michael straight out if he were the cause.

"Yes," the angel answered, "it is I who turned off

your television set. Yes, I did it in order to obtain your attention.

"You know that we will be with both of you during every second of your mission here upon Earth— a mission that is now coming into bloom toward the Christ Light. Worry not of the details of life. We shall handle those. Worry not of your abundance. We shall see to that as you do the work. Simply focus upon the task at hand.

"Simply be the messenger of Light that you have come to be, that is all you have to do. Simply be an example of love for those around you in your own existence. We shall not fail in the continuance of our work."

Lori Jean said that the television set always works perfectly fine after she has received the message at the computer that Michael wishes to transmit.

"After I'm finished typing the new information, we can turn the set back on—and it works as good as new. Sometimes Michael will even say something like, 'Now go back to watching the movie. Enjoy! Have Love! I am Lord Michael.'"

A Cheerful, Loving, Very Human Mystic

My wife Sherry and I have found our relationship with thirty-seven-year-old Lori Jean Flory to be truly blessed. Sweet of disposition with a cheerful personality, she is at first glance as far from the common conception of a mystic, a medium, or a channel as one can get. However, when she explains her lifepath in greater detail in Chapter One, we shall see that she is, indeed, spiritually well-assembled and wonderfully well-prepared for her Earth assignment. She most certainly is of the very stuff of which true mystics are made.

Supported on all levels by her husband Charles, who seems always to be a true and complete gentleman, Lori Jean lives a quiet existence totally permeated by a deep sense of her oneness with God, humankind, nature, and the universe.

Above all, with her abiding love of all things, she is undogmatic and unfailingly humble regarding her reception of these angelic messages.

After I had agreed to assist her in helping to distribute Michael's wisdom teachings to a wider audience, she spoke very frankly of her moments of self-examination and "human-ness."

In a fax dated February 21, 1995, Lori Jean confessed that sometimes she wondered if it were really Michael from whom she was receiving the lovely, inspirational messages.

"And yet," she added, "he always comes forth with words of confirmation. I know that I am *not* the only one receiving from Michael on the planet. *That is a fact!* I just occasionally wonder in my humanness, why me? Once Michael said that it was because I was a pure receiver."

Lori Jean has always stressed how important she believes it is to be humble in one's attitude toward working in partnership with the angels.

"I don't want any traces of my ego or personality showing up in any information that might come through me. Being humble is very important to me. I just want to step aside and be as clear as I can possibly be.

"I think this 'clearness' is why the angels began attuning me when I was only three—although I don't claim that I began to understand it all until I was about twenty-one."

She does not remember seeing the beings of light very often while the attunement process was being instrumented.

"It was more of a sensing, a feeling, a knowing that I did not figure out until I was much older."

When she was a child, the angelic beings did not encourage Lori Jean to speak to others about their interaction with her—and, she once said, it never occurred to her to do so.

"I surely did not feel that I was any more special than anyone else, but when I was a little girl, I would probably have been talked out of believing what was happening to me."

As an adult, Lori Jean understands and welcomes the angelic visitations.

"When I was around the age of three, however, I did not always understand or welcome the experiences.

"I did not know why I could not move my arms or legs when these attunements were taking place.

"I did not understand that when the sounds of angelic bells and their frequencies were rising to a crescendo that I was being taken out of my body. Sometimes this leaving the body and returning would take place more than once in a night.

"I did not see the gorgeous visions of angels that so many children have reported having seen as little ones. I have since been told by Daephrenocles that they were there, but I did not visually perceive them.

"Daephrenocles has also told me of the little entities that would come and play with me. I don't remember those, either.

"I *do* remember that sometimes—just like lots of kids—I would be afraid to let my toes stick out of the end of the bed at night."

Lori Jean does understand completely how blessed she was to have a good and loving family.

"I may have been a bit sheltered in a small town,

but I did not have to suffer the difficulties that so many others face. When I was a kid growing up, there were no problems with drugs, drinking, smoking, and so forth. I regularly experience the Other Side, but it has never been because of drugs, illness, or a near-death experience."

Lori Jean sought to explain to me more of her method, or technique, of receiving angelic messages.

"I will be quite honest with you. I am a conscious channel, not a deep trance, unconscious channel as is my friend Lois East—though I do seem to be moving in that direction.

"There really is no specific formula to what I do. I have no definite structure, rules, or wheres and whys. I just follow the intuition and inspirations that I am given.

"Daephrenocles once told me that when I came in this time, I was 'above average intuitive.' Others have informed me that I was one of the Greek Oracles long ago. I am told that I have done this kind of work so many times that it is almost as easy as falling off a log for me.

"There is no specific time each day that I receive messages. Again, that for me is strictly intuitive. Things work when they are supposed to.

"What often happens is that I will be going about whatever my human self needs to be doing. Michael

26

will begin putting images into my mind, like a preview of what he will want to talk about. But I have no idea of what he will say. How can I? I can't receive impressions and visions from him as I am going about doing regular, everyday things.

"If I don't get around to sitting down at the computer and receiving this particular message that he wishes to convey, he will continue to place the same image into my consciousness until I do sit down and allow his light to come through me. He doesn't hit me over the head, though. He is very loving, patient, and allowing.

"I sometimes meditate with music for a while, though nothing with me is absolute or set in stone.

"After I have been meditating for a few minutes, sometimes longer, and after I have prayed and surrounded myself with light, I begin to feel what seems like a waterfall of pure light descending upon me. It enters through the top of my head and whooshes through me. It feels as though every cell in my body has just been washed through clear and clean. Totally clear.

"Then, as I let go, the words, visions, and images begin to flow from Michael and my fingers begin to type.

"Most often, my eyes are closed—and I am wafting off somewhere else. *But I am still here.* If the telephone rings, I hear it—though sometimes Michael prevents that. But even then, *no one takes over my body*! It is more a case of Michael and my other guides bringing a band of light energy around my aura should any kind of physical disturbance manifest in my immediate environment. The angels simply assist with the energies, like a power-booster type of thing. And when I come out of it, I am ready to do something else."

ARCHANGEL MICHAEL, PRINCE OF THE HEAVENLY HOSTS

For many years now I have owned a small statue of the Archangel Michael brandishing his spear point at Satan's throat. This statue always sits either on my desk or directly behind me on a bookshelf.

I obtained the image at a gift shop when Sherry and I were visiting the Grotto of the Redemption in West Bend, Iowa. The Grotto has a life-size statue of Michael besting the devil on a tall column near its main entrance.

I bought the statue not only because Michael and the angels are very special to me, but because I was at the time experiencing some rather nasty negative manifestations in my office in our home in Paradise

Valley, Arizona. What began as a series of eerie thumps and bumps had progressed to books moving off shelves and my word processor printing out bizarre messages, sometimes in a totally foreign alphabet, such as Hebrew or Arabic—a talent far beyond my machine's normal capacity.

Almost immediately after I had placed the statue of Archangel Michael in my office, the annoying phenomena ceased. Sherry even managed to snap a photograph of a bright angelic being hovering over the keyboard of my word processor. In my opinion, the power of prayer, coupled with the angelic energy of Michael, managed to convince my uninvited guests to leave.

In the opinion of those skeptical to matters of the spirit, I am certain that the whole episode would seem to be simply a matter of the power of suggestion from onset to denouement.

It may be all well and good for the cynics to decry such supernatural experiences. Such materialistic challenges keep those of us who are aware of the unseen worlds on our toes.

And, of course, we stand ever-prepared to assist our worldly brothers and sisters in those instances when a sudden encounter with the unknown and the unexplainable shatters their fragile physical reality.

It is in such moments that they may be much more receptive to hearing more about the Archangel Michael and his ability to keep the minions of evil under his heel.

Just who is this Michael on whom I and millions of other angel adherents rely to keep devilish intruders at bay and from whom such contemporary mystics as Lori Jean Flory claim communication?

First and foremost, Michael is the Chief of God's armies, champion of the people of God in the Old Testament, and fierce guardian of God's chosen flock in the New Testament. He is most often represented in works of art as the mighty angel warrior, the conqueror of Satan, who sets his powerful heel upon the head of the insidious foe and threatens him with his sword, pierces him with his spear, or is prepared to chain him in the abyss at the sounding of Judgment Day's clear trumpet blast.

The Roman Catholic Church gives to Michael the highest position among the angels and refers to him as "Prince of the Heavenly Hosts." He is remembered in many portions of Catholic liturgy and is honored by two feasts.

According to some traditions, it was Michael who responded to Lucifer's rebellious angels in Heaven and who rallied God's loyal beings of light to cast out the disobedient ones. From that time on, all the angels of light recognize Michael as their captain and remain attentive to his every command.

Archangel Michael has long been acknowledged as the Guardian of the Hebrew Nation. It is generally accepted that it was Michael who was sent by God to guide the Israelites through the desert, and an ancient Jewish tradition states that it was Michael who contended with Satan over the body of Moses and who hid the prophet's tomb in order to keep his remains eternally safe from desecration.

During the Babylonian Captivity, the prophet Daniel knew that it was Michael, the great prince, who defended the Jewish people.

Michael is invoked as the principal defender of the synagogue. The Feast of the Atonement concludes with the following invocation: "Michael, prince of mercy, pray for Israel, that it may reign in heaven in that light which streams forth from the face of the King who sits upon the throne of mercy."

The Emperor Constantine credited his military victories to the protection of Michael and built a magnificent church near Constantinople in honor of the Archangel.

During the pontificate of St. Gregory the Great, a gigantic image of Michael appeared in the skies. With a thrust of his mighty sword, he ended the terrible plague that was ravaging the people of Rome.

Joan of Arc claimed assistance from Michael for her mission of aiding the French king to restore peace and prosperity to his kingdom.

In addition to his function as heaven's greatest military guardian, Michael is revered as a marvelous agent of healing. And when it is time for us to pass through the portal of physical death, it is Michael who will see us safely to the Light Eternal.

And, as the end of the present world draws near, it will be Michael who will lead the final battle against the Antichrist, who by false miracles and brilliant oratory, will seek to lure even the elect of God into the ranks of Satan's army. In that last, ultimate battle of the Children of Light against the Children of Darkness, Michael will once again best the prince of darkness and cast him into the abyss of hell.

Even with this brief dossier detailing the grandeur and might of Archangel Michael, we can surely understand Lori Jean Flory's reluctance to accept even the suggestion that such a supreme being of light might be asking her to receive his messages.

But as you will see for yourself as you experience the wisdom teachings shared by Michael through Lori Jean, the awesome Prince of the Heavenly Host has chosen to express words of love, light, and inspiration to help keep our souls afloat on the troubled waters of these most turbulent times.

It is the Michael of love, compassion, divine enlightenment, and healing who speaks to us in these chapters. And he speaks in simple language and metaphors of nature so that all might easily absorb the comfort and succor of his words.

A CALM IN THE CENTER OF THE STORM

On January 18, 1995, in meditation, Lori Jean was inspired to ask of Michael a special message of guidance as we agreed to focus our energies on the preparation of this book.

"As I tuned in," she said, "I sensed the presence of Michael standing directly behind me and observing me over my shoulders. He was wearing a radiant white robe with golden, satinlike material at the wrists of the sleeves. Around the edging of the sleeves was a darker golden color. He felt and looked radiant."

Herewith is Michael's message:

Beloved Ones, in the rushing of the winds of negativity that in these days confuses the lives of so many humans, know that there is a place of calm and love in the center of such turbulence and

33

chaos. We angels endeavor to bring all beloved souls into the place of peace that exists amidst the storms of everyday life. We seek lovingly to teach the Children of the One God that this haven of tranquillity exists within each heart and can always be attained with love. It is not necessary for you to be buffeted about by the many disturbing and disruptive outer forces of life.

The God Force sustains all, and it is constantly present to offer all-encompassing, unconditional love. It is such selfless love that shall carry each one of you safely along the path to the mountaintop.

The God Force contains only pure love—purer than those who cling to the ways of the earth plane can ever know. I wish gently to remind each of you Children of the One God that you are of pure love and pure light, which is always present within you.

Beloved Ones, I wish to bring forth on Earth that which has already been completed in the higher realms of heavenly light. I wish to share this knowing with the many of your kind, and the loving angels shall assist you each and every step of the way. All the beloved messengers of light are participating in the elevation of consciousness on your planet.

Listen only to the voices from the heavenly realms that speak to you within the silence of meditation.

Many are called, but few are chosen—because few choose themselves to be chosen by saying, "Yes, we will work with the heavenly realms."

With the help of the angels and the knowledge that we stand beside you and behind you, many shall move away from the shadows and into the light of God. Let us move forward!

With greatest love and blessings, I am, Michael.

CHAPTER ONE

*Living in Partnership
with the Angels*

Sometime early in 1988, my husband Charles and I attended a Divine Science Church where our friend Lois East was holding a channeling session after the formal service.

Later, a woman named Ella approached me and very matter-of-factly said, "Lori Jean Flory, all of your spiritual talents and abilities are about to open completely and fully. Some people have one or two gifts from God, but you have many! And they all are going to open. So many people are going to know of you that you will have to turn them away from your door."

I smiled, thanked the woman, and walked on with Charles. I'm just not one to get puffed up over such statements. I find it interesting that so many people have said similar things to me since 1980, but I just let it go in one ear and out the other.

All of us are unfolding. I know I will be for a long time. Each of us should always be discovering new things about ourselves and one another.

I have often stated that I feel no need to be right. Charles and I both feel only a great responsibility to be as light-filled as we possibly can be. We will follow only those pathways that give evidence of truth and integrity. We have reverence for God's plan and the light that shines in all of us.

It is also very important to me that people understand that I have no desire to influence them into accepting my pathway as their own or to impose my truth upon them. I respect other people's philosophies and points of view.

I always tell people that the truth is within themselves and not in the words of any other person. Each person's truth is valid and each is different—yet all are a part of the one.

If I argued with people or if I tried to convince them that *my* way was the *only* way, then I would not be expressing reverence for the light that shines within them.

We Each Have One Foot in Spirit, the Other on Earth

Because of my lifelong experiences with the Other Side, I am convinced that we are all beautiful, powerful, spiritual divine beings who are adjusting to life experiences in a human body.

Both aspects of ourselves are important. We should enjoy our human bodies, but the true challenge on Earth is to integrate our physical selves and our spiritual selves. Each of us has one foot in spirit and the other on Earth. And sometimes that can be quite a stretch!

But I believe that we are magnificent *now*, enlightened *now*, and divine *now*. We don't necessarily need to climb to the mountaintop to have a guru give us our truth. All we have to do is to learn to look within ourselves and listen. The answers are there.

In my sincere and earnest opinion, I believe that the truths in this book were written by Archangel Michael in the higher spheres of light long before I ever knew that I would receive the assignment to convey them into the written word. And I am certainly not suggesting that I was selected for this work because of any great merit or acquired spiritual gifts on my part. The *why* of how I came to be so blessed by Michael is as much of a mystery to me as it may be to others.

Born into a Home Filled with Love

I was born in a small California town on September 21, 1957, the second of four children. My brother Kent was the first born; Nancy, the third; Owen is the baby.

There was a lot of love in our home, and all my life I have felt truly blessed to have the parents that I have. I was loved as a child and never abused. I was told often how much I was wanted. I believe every child needs to feel wanted and to hear such loving words.

My father has been an attorney since 1954. Mom has her lifetime teaching credentials. They recently celebrated their fortieth wedding anniversary. I am very proud of them.

No family is perfect. Every family has its ups and downs, but I feel blessed to have had the parents I had. I chose well.

I will never forget something wonderful that my parents would always do at Christmastime. They would put together a large box of clothes, food, candies, fruits, and other goodies—and just show up unannounced at the doorstep of some poor family. My parents taught me kindness and love for others, which opened and broadened my heart.

I graduated from high school in 1975, attended junior college for one year, and received my BA degree in liberal arts from California Lutheran University in 1979.

My Earth Mission: Being of Service to God

Such a solid background would seem to be the very epitome of middle-class American normalcy. And certainly I give every appearance of being completely normal in every way. You see, I just do not think it unusual to be able to converse with angelic beings on a regular basis.

My main spiritual guidance, the angel Daephrenocles, has told me that my spiritual purpose in being born upon Earth was to be of service to God.

In 1988, I was given my angelic or soul name, "Alaeyash," which means, "Soothing Flower of Light." One's soul name describes the essence of the soul or the energy vibration that is known to God.

I am very close to Daephrenocles. His vibration of energy is to me like the knock on the door by a welcome friend.

While it is true that angels are androgynous beings, balanced in their female and male energies, Daephrenocles appears to me as a male representation of his spirit energies.

Angels and masters can appear in many different ways. What is important to them is that we are comfortable relating with them so that a solid relationship may commence to grow. When this occurs, then those beings of light are able to grow as well. It is a reciprocal thing.

I have been told that before my birth it was agreed between my soul and the master beings of Light all around me that during my lifetime there would be a pathway, a blueprint, a road map if you will, that I must travel.

I don't remember much of my life before the age of three except for my spiritual experiences, which I recall as though they occurred yesterday.

Interestingly, I don't ever remember talking to anyone in my family about these experiences—nor does any member of my family remember me ever having said anything about such angelic encounters. I think that they occurred so often that I came to take them for granted. I simply thought that everyone had such experiences, so no big deal.

Also, on a spiritual level, I don't think the angels wanted me to discuss my experiences with them. As in so many families, my loving parents might have tried to convince me that I was imagining everything.

Undergoing a Process of Spiritual Attunement

I remember very well the angelic process of attunement that began when I was but a child of three.

After my little head would nestle into my pillow, I would hear one or two of the sweetest ringings of a little bell that you can imagine. My eyes were always closed when these experiences would occur— and throughout my life, I have most often kept my eyes closed during spiritual encounters.

With the sound of the bell would come a buzzing sound. It would start at a low pitch and keep raising higher and higher in frequency and sound. I would feel as though I was being lifted up by the increasing sound, then lowered as the sound became lower.

I did not know that I was having out-of-body experiences then. I could never move a limb during these experiences until the pitch would come back down.

When the attunement process was over, I would again hear the very sweet angelic bell ring once or twice.

As Daephrenocles has explained to me, I agreed to undergo this process of attunement before I came into this life.

Understand, though, that during the day I was just a regular kid, running around and having fun. I also

43

want to make it clear that I never knew when the sessions would occur—but they did occur often. Sometimes three or four in one night.

I never saw the angels with my physical eyes. I *knew* someone or something was there with me, but I never actually saw them. I *felt* and *heard*.

Such experiences continued throughout my childhood and on through my teenage and young adult years. I know now that the attunement process that occurred here on Earth meant that on the higher, finer, etheric spiritual levels, all the levels of my being, the layers of my aura—my light body—were also being attuned. This was done so that the Light Beings and I could work together at a later age.

As I entered my twenties, the attunement process seemed to widen into another kind of experience that would most often occur while I would be resting or falling asleep. I was always conscious, so I know that they were not dreams. They were higher dimensional attunement kind of experiences.

What would occur is that I would feel what felt like a laser beam of light energy focused at my third eye area in my forehead. These focused bursts of light would open my third eye—or where the inner vision is focused, the sight of the soul, so to speak. I would see white light, and I would experience what felt like a wind tunnel. I would be aware that I was stepping into the Other Side.

During one such experience, which occurred in my thirties, I emerged from a tunnel of light into a white garden arbor with roses beyond it. The roses emitted music and harmony, as well as fragrance, in praise to God.

I was about to walk through this beautiful arbor when I heard a loud voice say, *"Go back!"*

I opened my eyes, back in my physical body, in reverent awe of what had just transpired.

Acquiring a Solid Spiritual Foundation

I can recall sitting in church as a child and very often seeing pastel beings of light flowing around the pulpit in the midst of the service.

I knew about angels, of course, but I did not connect them to my experiences. I have never once in my life doubted the existence of God, but when I was a child I can't say that I knew that I had a personal guardian angel. Remember that I had only felt and heard, not seen, the entities around me during my attunement. To me at that time, angels were just beautiful beings that I saw in books.

I grew up and was confirmed in the American Lutheran Church. Our family went to church every Sunday, and I always attended Sunday school before the church services.

I think that through the years this gave me a very good, solid spiritual foundation. Mom taught Sunday school, and sometimes I would get up in front of the class to help her teach.

Later, I also taught Sunday school and vacation Bible school. I couldn't have guessed then that one day I would be a teacher on a bit more unconventional spiritual path.

Learning Respect for Nature and All of Life

As I have emphasized, my childhood was happy, innocent, and filled with love.

Dad blessed us kids with two horses and a pony, and we were allowed to ride as far and as long as we wanted whenever we wished. Dad had had horses when he was a child, and his father had ridden show jumpers.

I became known as the "Horse Kid," because I was always drawing pictures of horses. And through *Western Horseman* magazine, I eventually acquired fifty pen pals who loved horses as much as I did.

My horse Spud was my best friend when I was a kid, and we spent many hours together riding through the hills. Dad had a horse named Napoleon, and we often rode together.

We were taught respect of nature and the animals and birds. Our reverence for nature was increased on weekend hikes and bike rides with Dad. Looking back, I can see that he helped me to be sensitive to Mother Nature and all that she encompasses.

I believe that my love of animals only served to open me even more to those so subtle and etheric energies around us that issue from the other side of the veil.

Learning Necessary Lessons for Soul Growth

When I reflect upon my childhood and teenage years, I know that I could never have been thought of as a "social butterfly." I was always more of a loner, often more to myself. To put it another way, I guess that you might say that I was "socially uncoordinated," and I was teased a lot by the other kids.

I wasn't really a popular kid always at parties and going out on dates. I was more into artistic and intuitive pursuits. I spent hours with our horses, riding through the hills, contemplating, thinking, observing nature. I think that having cats, dogs, chickens, and horses and raising and showing lambs as a member of Future Farmers of America did much to teach me responsibility for all creatures.

The first time that I wore any makeup was in the seventh grade. And that only happened because before homeroom a bunch of girls hauled me into the girls' room and saw to it that I started using at least a little makeup. Of course the boys in homeroom noticed the change right away and began to tease me.

I have always loved to sing, and I was a member of choirs in junior high, high school, church, and college. I especially enjoyed singing in Handel's *Messiah*.

When I was in high school, I learned to play the piano—and I actually became quite good. For two or three years I provided the musical accompaniment for various ceremonies and meetings of Job's Daughters, a church service group for women.

My days in high school were not particularly filled with pleasant experiences. I knew that I was not that popular with the other students—and from time to time my self-esteem dipped pretty low.

Growing up in a small town gave me roots, a sense of who I was, but it also provided me with some rather tough lessons in humility and getting along with others. In a small town where everyone knows everyone else, where students stay together from kindergarten through high school graduation, one can get typecast at an early age and be judged as different from childhood to adulthood—or however long one stays in that limited social environment.

As I look back on those times, I can see that I was undergoing lessons that made me who I am today. All those experiences were necessary for growth on a soul level.

As I have acknowledged, the Lutheran Church gave me a good spiritual foundation, but I always felt that there was something missing. Traditional religion and its attendant dogma did not completely satisfy me or give me a sense of fulfillment. It wasn't until my senior year in college that I truly began to come together on all levels of being.

THE COMING OF DAEPHRENOCLES

It was between my junior and senior year at California Lutheran University in Thousand Oaks, California, that I underwent a number of growth experiences that prepared me for my first conscious interaction with the angel Daephrenocles.

An Invisible Presence Keeps Me from Falling Over a Cliff

The summer of 1978, I worked in the beauty of Yellowstone National Park. The surroundings were perfect for someone such as me to be energized and healed by Mother Nature herself. I lived in Canyon Village, about a quarter of a mile from the "Grand Canyon of the Yellowstone." I washed dishes and cleaned cabins, but I also backpacked, hiked, and absorbed the spectacular natural elegance that is Yellowstone.

I also slipped backward while hiking and could have fallen over the cliff and plunged to my death in the rapids of the Yellowstone River far below.

A friend who was hiking with me managed to grab hold of me and pull me back up to solid ground. I *knew* that there had been an invisible presence all around me that had kept me from falling.

To say that I would be grateful to God and the angels forever would be an understatement.

Meeting Two Valuable Catalysts on the Path

Back at college, I shared a small room with three other students.

When four young women are placed in tight quarters and asked to live together, many personality conflicts are bound to arise. It seemed that I had much Karma to resolve in this area.

To compensate for "personality conflicts under crowded conditions," I found a true friend and confidante in Kathleen Meyer, the woman for whom I was baby-sitting.

Upon our very first meeting, we connected as though our friendship had always been meant to be. We discovered that we both had interests in common, especially in metaphysical teachings.

Before my discussions with Kathleen, I was not consciously aware of the identity of the various beings of light. I simply knew they were there.

At that point, I had begun to see concentrated flashes of light and to hear light frequencies on an almost daily basis. It was as though it was all a part of a divine plan that, finally, at the age of twenty-one, I would begin to understand what had been occurring in my life for eighteen years. Soon, I was learning to identify and name certain beings of light by the colors that I saw surrounding them.

Kathleen began also to introduce me to techniques for receiving messages from the angelic beings.

I knew that I had been communicating somehow, but now I was able to be clearer about the process.

I must also give much credit for my spiritual awakening to Joseph Gregory, a friend of Kathleen, who was one of the most spiritual people I have ever known. Joseph had a powerful impact on my spiritual growth. Like Kathleen, he helped me to understand things that had been going on in my life ever since I had been a small child. This dear man passed to the other side in October 1988.

A Master Teacher Manifests in a Restaurant

Then came that remarkable moment when I was in a restaurant with Kathleen and her two children and a voice—certainly not Kathleen's—suddenly came through the young mother with a message for me.

The angelic being identified himself as a master teacher, and he said that he had walked with me, talked with me, listened to me, and had often held my hand.

When Kathleen returned to full consciousness, she told me that she had been aware of the entity standing next to my left side at the table and she said that this particular teacher wanted to give me his name.

Kathleen went on to say that he was a highly evolved being of light and that I should meditate and learn the entity's name for myself.

I remember sitting in my dorm room on campus trying to do just that. It was so frustrating, because

I kept getting two names that were being whispered to me—"Daephren" and "Daeocles."

Upon our next meeting, Kathleen helped me to receive the correct name, *Daephrenocles.*

This occurred in the fall of 1978, right after I had turned twenty-two. The Master Teacher Daephrenocles had appeared—and I, the student, was ready for him. He told me that it was time to get on with the business of stripping away the veils from my vision and memory.

Learning to Listen to Daephrenocles's Whispers of Wisdom

It was also at this time that my spiritual hearing began to open more, as well. I began to hear Daephrenocles whisper to me in my left ear in response to questions.

At first, I would hear only a "yes" or a "no," but as time passed, his answers evolved into words, then sentences, then paragraphs, and then complete running conversations.

Receiving "Laser" Bursts of Light and Visions

Later, "laser" bursts of light within my third eye began to manifest words and letters of light in the form of visions. These bursts of light would also trigger out-of-body experiences.

I would, however, often keep my spiritual eyes closed, and I would *sense* and *hear* more than I would see while out of my body.

Spiritual Awareness Is a Process of Steady Unfoldment

I have undergone a steady process of spiritual unfoldment over many years. When some people approach me and say that they want to receive from the angels as I do, *overnight, instantly,* I tell them that it just doesn't work that way.

Even a car has to speed up one mile at a time. It can't do 0–70 in two seconds. The transmission has to shift into its various gears. Right?

So it has been with me. One mile at a time.

THE ANGELS OF LOVE BRING MY TWIN SOUL

Early in 1980, the year after I graduated from college, I received a telephone call from a psychic friend who told me the following rather exciting news:

"Your true love is coming. He is not here yet. Right

now he is involved with someone, and he is growing spiritually. He is learning specific lessons, as is the woman with whom he is currently involved.

"You are growing and learning lessons as well. When your true loves comes, you will feel like following him wherever he goes.

"Do not run after the first man that you meet that you might think is he, your true love.

"If you rush a relationship, there will be a divorce.

"If you learn your lessons, you will meet your true love when you are twenty-five.

"If you do not learn your lessons, you will not meet him until you are fifty."

As my destiny would have it, I had not learned enough real-life lessons. The marriage that I entered in September 1982 quickly deteriorated beyond any hope of salvation.

Obviously, the two of us each had lessons to learn from the other—but equally obviously, he was not my true love.

On August 10, 1983, I walked into the office that an astrologer, Charles Flory, shared with a psychic-sensitive and hypnotherapist named George Gillette. Charles and I soon became "friendly acquaintances."

In September, when I turned twenty-five, I got a job teaching preschool in Fresno. In November, I filed for divorce.

As Christmas approached, I decided to write down all of my feelings about Charles Flory, my "friendly acquaintance."

I was amazed when it took me two full pages to get everything down.

And then I decided to do something daring. I would call Charles and read my feelings to him over the telephone. If he rejected me, well, at least I had expressed myself and I could move on.

The next morning I called him at his office, and we talked for two hours. Charles did not reject me, but he did seem startled to learn how I felt about him.

"Uh-oh," he said when I told him of my feelings.

" 'Uh-oh, I'm rejected?' " I asked.

"No," he replied. "Just, uh-oh, I'm surprised!"

As the days went by, I discovered that Charles had been attracted to me for quite some time and that he would have pursued me more actively if it had not been for his knowledge of my divorce proceedings and his own uncertain marital situation. We exchanged a holiday kiss, then began seeing each other regularly after December 19.

One day in January, when I was visiting Charles in his office, I began to speak to him of the angels.

Although he had an extensive background in metaphysics, he had never really thought much about guardian angels or guides.

The angels asked me to have Charles face me in his chair and to have our knees touching. Next, they instructed him to touch my fingertips very lightly.

I relaxed, breathed deeply, and began to lift my consciousness. Then I simply let go and allowed the words to come through.

The angels told Charles that it was time for him to get on with his life and to stop allowing himself to be abused and manipulated. It was time to feel good about his work as an astrologer and to tolerate no longer those who made fun of him.

They went on to tell him that it was time to begin loving himself and to stop the suffering that he had been feeling.

The angels did not tell him what to do, they simply made suggestions to stop the suffering that he had been feeling for so long. The angelic energies were peaceful and harmonious.

When I opened my eyes and beheld Charles's face, I could see at once that his troubled expression had been transmuted to one of peace.

Although I had been receiving the angelic vibrations since I was three years old, this was the first formal reading that I had ever given to anyone.

Afterward, Charles asked me to lunch. I was a little shy and nervous, as it had been quite a while since

I had been in any kind of positive situation with a man. I didn't quite know what to say or how to act— but it was fun! Charles still thanks the angels for that day.

In October 1984, Charles and I moved together to Colorado Springs. Charles got a job working in an alcohol detox facility, as well as managing an apartment complex. I went to school to become a travel agent.

In April 1985, we moved to Denver where Charles had a position working in a shelter for abused teens and I secured a job in a travel agency. We were married on July 28, 1985.

My psychic friend's prediction had proved accurate. I had rushed into my first serious relationship and marriage and it had ended in divorce. At the same time, through that awful experience, I truly did learn some difficult life lessons—thus I was able to meet my true love when I was twenty-five and did not have to wait until I was fifty!

Daephrenocles had worked to bring us together. He once told me that the angels would have kept pulling us around until we came together—no matter how long it would take!

He said that Charles and I are like two white horses prancing together. He said that we are like

10x10 and not 1+1. We are doing our spiritual work together, and we work as a team.

After more than ten years together, we are still very much in love. The words in our house are *us*, *ours*, and *we*, not *I*, *me*, and *you*.

MY PARTNERSHIP WITH THE ANGELS ACCELERATES WITH THE MANIFESTATION OF ARCHANGEL MICHAEL

In January 1988, I began to receive messages from Daephrenocles through the process of automatic writing while sitting at the keyboard of my typewriter. In June, I was beginning to become known in the Denver area for my angelic readings, and by 1989, Charles and I were publishing our *Enchanted Spirits* newsletter.

In October 1993 when the Heavenly Prince became insistent that we begin work on the book of wisdom teachings, I started to keep a kind of journal of running commentary. As I reflect back on my entries, I see that many of my remarks are quite revelatory of the entire process of angelic communication, and I have chosen to quote a number of select excerpts at this point in the text:

November 13, 1993

The past couple of days I have not been able to work on the book. The first day it seemed I was giving readings all day that I didn't know I would be doing. . . . Yesterday I was working on the newsletter. . . . I feel Michael wants to keep to a schedule of doing the work each morning. I had an inner vision of him yesterday afternoon when I caught a quick nap. It seems that if I miss too much time, more than a day . . . he will remind me that we must keep on schedule. It is almost an endearing thing.

November 15 . . . 10:30 A.M.

This morning when I sat down to meditate prior to allowing the words for the book to flow through, I felt or sensed in my open cupped hands a beautiful pink rose, fully bloomed that turned white. I also felt hands of light working on my head, chakras, and third eye—this I tangibly felt before the words began to flow and the typing began.

November 20 . . .

I have been a bit late this week doing the book. Everything has been so busy it seems. I have been seeing Michael at night appearing in my inner vision. . . . I am also seeing Light Beings more clearly with outer vision. I saw Michael's portrait wink at me.... I am glad that he is patient.

November 29 ...

This morning after seeing Charles off to work at 5:30 A.M., I meditated.... I saw myself flowing out into space and looking at planet Earth. Letting go and surrendering allows us to have access to the big picture.... I saw a large group of beautiful Light Beings ... all in a circle, holding hands, focusing energy....

Within the circle was what at first seemed to be ... a rough "meteorite" or something.... Then it became less physical and became a sphere of light and something or someone was emerging from the light.... I felt an immense shift occur within my own third eye at this point....

December 10 ...

This morning I asked mentally of the angels, "Are you *sure* I am the one you want to do this book?"

I audibly heard a voice say, "You are the one."

Okay. I accept that. I also heard angelic bells three or four times.

December 27 ...

Over the Holidays, I had not quite as much time as I would have liked to work on the manuscript. Last night I heard an audible male voice (undoubtedly Michael's) say one word: *"Cooperate!"*

... I told him my intent has never been not to cooperate.... Now that the holidays are behind us, I should have more time ... on a daily basis....

December 29 ...

This evening Charles and I were in the living room ... watching some award show with Angela Lansbury speaking about the theater. All of a sudden the TV went dead, but none of the rest of the house was affected.

Charles asked if I touched the remote. I laughed and said, NO. I knew it was Michael trying to get my attention because I had not worked on the book today. I almost expected an angel to appear and begin to scold us. Then the TV went back on as perfectly normal as you please.

So I went ahead and worked on the book....

When the television went dark, I felt an immense amount of powerful energy around me, a VERY high energy....

January 22, 1994

Lately I have been seeing a brilliant sphere of Golden-White Light that has been appearing over my

head when I have opened my eyes from meditations
and prayers. . . .

I Am Just an Instrument of the Angels

Cocreating this book has increased my own growth
and self-confidence, though I suppose I will never
feel totally worthy of working with a being like Archangel Michael.

I was brought up to be humble and to always keep
my feet on the ground. To know what is in the heart
is far more important than the scope of material
things that one may or may not acquire in life. Love
is what you take with you when you pass over, not
material possessions. The real reason that we are here
on Earth is to grow spiritually. We are not on this
planet to enter a competition to see how much we
can amass. We are here to learn balance, to live with
one foot on Earth and the other in spirit.

Please remember that the wisdom teachings that I
have received constitute "Michael's book," not my
own thoughts.

I am just an instrument of the angels. I know that
there is always a danger in meditation that the
human ego and personality can filter through. I pray
that I have always properly stepped aside to let Mi-

chael speak through me without any interference on my part.

I also know that when I have meditated and focused on being the best that I can be for Michael, there have been those unseen others, who have helped me with a boosting of my light energies. It is as Jesus said, "It is the Father through me who doest these things, and not I."

I am in partnership with the angels, with the Light. I could never receive this way on my own. And I guess the angels need people like me to receive the words so that other hearts may be blessed.

I just want to add that we are all instruments of the Light, and I am no more special than anyone else. I am just me. All I can do is be the best me that I know how to be.

Experience the Love and the Wisdom of Michael for Yourself

As my friend Brad Steiger edited the wisdom teachings of Archangel Michael, he endeavored to set them forth in a manner in which all readers may truly feel as though Michael is speaking directly and personally to them.

Brad retained the endearment of "Beloved One," with which Michael so often greeted me, so that all readers will be able to experience the warmth of this salutation and sense the energies of love and blessing that I felt flow through my physical being as I received his words to share in this book.

It is my earnest hope that each reader will feel as though the Heavenly Prince is speaking directly to him or her and will come to experience the same joyful blessing of love, wisdom, and knowledge, and the same miracle of oneness with angelic intelligence that came to pass for me when I heeded the powerful voice of Archangel Michael that told me, "I want you!"

CHAPTER TWO

❦

Centering Within the Christ Light

Beloved One, to center within the Christ Light is to center within your own being.

Within the heart of the Christ Light lies the truth of who you really are and where your divinity truly resides.

The true light of the Christ within awaits patiently for you to awaken to it and to recognize its beauty.

It is the God Light within you.

It is the eternal light glowing ever bright.

It is the Golden Flame that never goes out.

It is the fountain of light within the heart that fills you with the peace that surpasses all understanding.

When you center within the Christ Light—the infinite, eternal connection to God within your heart—you live in harmony and are at peace within.

You have been awakened to the beauty of the Source of All, the One Light that encompasses all.

You have achieved an inner knowing that can come only from the heart.

Such a process of awakening and awareness may always elude the intellectual mind.

Be Like Unto a Beauteous Rosebud Opening and Blooming

To center within the Christ Light is to be like a golden, fragrant center of a rose blooming within your heart.

It is to allow the true spiritual fragrance of yourself to waft in the breezes of life to all other souls.

To center with the Christ Light is to know that you have become like a wondrous, beauteous rosebud that opens and blooms.

It is to be one with the knowing that the soft petals of the rose open in God's perfect light and time.

It is to be aware that the dewdrops that fall upon rose petals are like pearls of wisdom that are bestowed upon you in your moments of quiet meditation and reflection.

To center with the Christ Light is to allow the beautiful rose that you are to be filled with the Golden Light flowing in, through, and around you and to be one with the wondrous rays of sunshine that warm you and nurture you.

It is to transmute all cares, worries, and concerns into heavenly hands.

It is to rise above the mediocrities of the day and to know that there is a Higher Force to carry you through each moment that you are on Earth.

It's Wonderful to Be Human!

Beloved One, know always that your True Essence, your God Light, is of pure love and of pure light.

Allow the true gift and blessing of your own self to flow forward as a blessing to all other beings—human or animal.

Allow yourself to open your heart to healing, to light, to love, and to divinity.

In God's Light, you are first divine, then human—wondrously, beautifully human.

And it is wonderful to be human!

Join the Dance of Love and Light

To center within the Christ Light is to allow the dance of love and light within your heart to flow freely. It is to allow yourself to feel the kindness, the grace, the smiles to radiate outward.

Beloved One, picture now in your mind the image

of a dancer bedecked in colorful ribbons moving gracefully in rhythm, allowing the streamers to flow through the air.

See yourself joining hands with the dancer and permitting your hearts to meld together in one continuous flow of love and light.

Lift up your hands, palms upraised, and receive the golden light of that which encompasses all light and all love.

Know within your heart that there is a common rhythm that flows through all things on Earth.

Be aware that you and your sweet planet are interconnected, like beautiful flowing ribbons, gracefully wafting in the breezes of life.

Permit these ribbons to flow freely and do not entangle them in day-to-day pettiness or competitiveness.

Know that love is all that matters and know that your essence is of love.

The Christ Light Is Being Felt More and More on Earth

The Christ Light, the Purity of God, is a healing, regenerative, loving energy—and it is being felt more and more upon your planet.

The Christ Light is transmuting, purifying, and

cleansing millions of souls who have begun to open their hearts to the truth that they are so much more than they behold in their mirrors.

Be fully aware, Beloved One, that there is now a continual flow of waves of the Christ Light moving upon Earth nearly every month, and the consciousness of many is being raised even higher.

All over the planet, more and more people are thinking about their role as loving tenants of the Earth. Brave and courageous souls are not sitting idly by any longer. They are doing something about the many issues that affect the planet that has served all its inhabitants so steadfastly and so well for millennia.

We of the Angelic Forces will assist aware humans to do their part to help Mother Earth.

See the Beauty of God in Every Living Thing

When one centers in the Christ Light, there is a knowing of the oneness of all things and an awareness that all things are an expression of God.

Maintain this practice in your daily life:

Silently bless those whom you meet during your waking hours.

Look deeply into their eyes and see the Christ

Light that is behind their eyes, awaiting the opportunity to awaken fully.

See the beauty of God in every living thing.

The Christ Light within each heart is all encompassing and unconditional.

The Christ Light Brings the Realization that All Humanity Is One

The Christ Light that is awakening those millions of souls is bringing with it the realization that all humanity is one.

As people are being energized and enlivened, they become aware that so many things that have brought them fear and prejudice are but illusions. Such wisdom causes such negative feelings to lose their power.

Remember Who You Really Are

Beloved One, above and beyond all the experiences of the outer world exists the Real You—a sparkling being of light whom you may have forgotten.

It is now time to remember who you really are.

In the process of centering within the Christ Light, Beloved One, know that you are allowing yourself to be uplifted beyond the appearances and the vibrations of the everyday world in which you frequently find yourself immersed.

You are rising above pettiness and competition. You are becoming like a gentle, pure drop of celestial rain to wash away the pain and to cleanse the hearts of others.

You are becoming one with a higher vibration of love that can transmute hearts hardened by ego and the struggle for survival on Earth.

Humanity thirsts for love and peace within.

Take Time to Remember Your Special Blessings

Remember that in the eyes of God you are a very special being.

Do not fail to set aside time to appreciate the many gifts and blessings that you have received from the world in which you live.

Glory in the beauty of a sunrise and a sunset; a meadow flower and its sweet fragrance; the smell of a new puppy and the kisses that it bestows upon your face; the laughter and innocence of a child; and the child within each adult.

Allow the angels who are with you to uplift and enlighten you. They hear your prayers and pleas.

All you need to do is to ask them to open your

heart to love and to assist you to "bloom" wherever it is that you have been "planted."

Love Can Eliminate Fear and Regain Paradise

Remember that fear is an illusion, an untruth that may burst into great power in the mass consciousness.

To center in the Christ Light is to fine tune your heart so that it will respond like an angelic harp to the vibrations of peace and love.

Love is the most powerful force in the Universe, and if humans would learn to love each other—one person at a time—they could make the world a paradise.

When you are centered in the Christ Light, you know within the chambers of your heart that all humanity is one, even though individuals may awaken to God's love at different times and travel different pathways to truth.

Join the Collective Stream of God's All-Encompassing Love

Be a drop of water in the universal stream of God's all-encompassing love.

Is it not true that it takes each drop of water together to create the stream?

To make the stream complete, each drop of water must meld with the other.

As the stream rushes through the landscapes of life—the lush forest, the arid desert, the mountain boulders—it comes home eventually to the ocean.

In the Christ Light, all hearts are as one—and all come home to the vast ocean of consciousness that is God.

The Christ Light Radiates from Your Heart

Raising your consciousness is the key to higher awareness, but the process must first begin within your heart. The Christ Light is always there, abiding within the home of your heart, waiting to awaken you to its presence.

It matters not who you are or what you have done in your life, the Christ Light is within you, awaiting your awareness of its presence.

The One Truth

On Earth, all is illusion except for one truth: In the eyes of God, you are pure love and pure light.

Before you entered this life, you were light.

When you depart this life, you shall continue on as light.

Even as your soul expresses through your human body, you are light.

Although many illusions exist in the outer world of materiality, when one makes the transition to the higher worlds, one returns to the body of pure light, which is androgynous and has no color, creed, culture, or race.

It Is Now Time to Come Together in Love

All polarities of fear must cease—pettiness, jealousy, hatred, greed, bigotry, and racism.

All these negative forces that oppose love are illusions that stem from fear.

Center into the Christ Light within your heart where nothing can exist but love.

I, Archangel Michael, and all of the angelic host stand ready to assist all humans with love—if only they request our assistance for the highest good of all concerned.

It is now time for all humanity to come together in love.

Find Your Divinity in the Calm of Meditation and Prayer

Beloved One, know that there is no one single way to meditate.

There is no one way to drink of the pure waters within your soul.

Allow the waters of your soul within to be calm.

Be silent and drink deeply of the divinity within you.

When you are calm and your mind is quiet, the reflections within are clear. You do not need an outer voice to instruct you—unless you wish it to be so. Know that enlightenment exists within you now.

In the silence of meditation and prayer, reflect clearly on the calm lake of your soul, and you shall find your divinity.

Beloved One, you may have heard the words, "Be still and know that I am God."

Within your soul, you are of divinity and infinity.

As a part of God, there are aspects of you that are divine and infinite. When you fully comprehend this, you shall realize that each person travels an individual spiritual path and that each one's soul growth is unique and different.

The Steadfast Light of God

Within the center core of each star is a mighty source of light. This wondrous warmth and life-giving light flows outward in ever-widening arcs of radiance.

In like manner does the Christ Light open within your heart and move out in wider and wider circles to other hearts upon the Earth.

You know how wonderful the warmth of the Sun feels upon your physical being. The same effect is felt by the inner sun within your heart.

When you are centering within the Light of God, the warmth also radiates to all parts of your body and your being, bringing with it balance and healing on mental, emotional, and physical levels.

Are not the very stars steadfast in their positions in the heavens?

Do not the paths of the Sun and the Earth follow their precise routes in the cosmos?

Yes, of course.

Then is not the very light of God always steadfast within the chambers of your own heart as well?

Yes, it is. It is always loving, always uplifting, always emanating healing energy—when you are open to receive it.

What Are the Benefits of Centering Within the Christ Light?

A sense of calm and an enlightened perspective into life's daily events.

A feeling of inner peace in the midst of chaos.

A knowing that you are being surrounded with serenity and light.

Great inner clarification as you learn to listen within your own heart.

A certainty that you are never alone, that many angelic beings are assisting you.

The assurance—felt from the heart, not the intellect—that you are a part of God and that God is a part of you.

The awareness that no matter what is occurring in your life, God is a constant—and the light within your heart is waiting to shine forth from your eyes, your smile, your compassion, and your gentle love.

You know that you have the ability to touch others with your radiance, thus bringing about shifts in their life experiences as well.

When you center within the Christ Light, you feel the connectedness, the grace, and the gentleness of nature. And you perceive that there is no separation between you and nature, and therefore, no separation between you and God.

It is as if you are standing on a mountaintop with arms outstretched, palms up, receiving the light full into your being.

When you center within the Christ Light, you will find that it is as if you have risen above the thick fog of illusion of life on Earth.

You are now high on a hilltop, observing the fog, but no longer being confused within it.

From this elevated vantage point, you can now see your lifepath much more clearly and determine what specific actions may need to be taken to avoid traps and mires on the road ahead.

The elegance that you will feel when centered within the Christ Light in your meditations is beyond physical words.

It is a peace that permeates one's very being.

It is a knowing that there is a special place on the planet where the vibrations are pure and high. That special place is within your heart wherever you are— for you and the oneness of God are connected at all times within the pure force of love.

CHAPTER THREE

☙

Angels Are Wayshowers

To use poetic imagery, one might say that life is like a beautiful, winding, light-filled white staircase of spiritual growth and lessons from God.

Step by step, you humans grow and learn, and we angels ascend with you—for we have within us the awareness and knowledge of God's wisdom.

Beloved One, we angels see so clearly the immense number of hearts upon your planet who are suffering and who are in pain.

We see the need for all humans to awaken to the awareness that they are children of God and therefore have the right to be touched with the Light of God.

We angels are the Wayshowers, the guides upon the stairs of life that lead you to the awareness of God's love.

The Flower Garden of Humanity

Beloved One, visualize a daisy in your mind.

Sometimes it seems to us angels as if you humans are wondrous wildflowers growing in a vast field of many, many thousands of your kind. Just like a many-petaled daisy, these petals, these individual aspects, grow from one center, one source—God.

Many daisies create one hillside of yellow and gold light-filled flowers, all rooted within the earth, all reaching up toward the Sun.

In like manner, you and your fellow humans are like a multitude of daisies, rooted on Earth, all reaching for the one source of light within your hearts—God.

Look to your fellow humans with love in your heart and compassion in your being.

Know that you are one with all.

As flowers of humanity, let the sunshine, the golden Light of God flow upon you and through you and provide nourishment for your spiritual growth.

You know how warm and loving the spring sunshine seems after a long, harsh winter. You know the joy that you feel when you see the buds on tree branches and the wildflowers in the fields beginning to blossom.

From our perspective as angels, we see humanity

81

in the process of awakening from a spiritual sleep and beginning to emerge and bloom.

And just as the Sun helps the plants to grow, so does the Christ Light that shines in each accepting heart assist humans to grow in spiritual strength and stature.

We Come to Lift You High Upon the Wings of Your Hearts

In your quiet, meditative moments, allow love to radiate from your heart to any person or thing.

Mentally or audibly affirm the following: "There is only the God Presence, the Christ Light, centered in this [person, animal, bird, insect, etc.]."

Beloved One, we, the Angelic Messengers of God, come to you with the greatest love and reverence in our hearts for you.

We come to love.

We come to uplift.

We come to enliven.

We wish only to add joy and a higher consciousness to each human.

We come to lift you high upon the very wings of your own hearts.

You are the love that you desire.

You are the light that you seek.

Love and light are to be found within.

You are the healer and the healing that you seek.

The physician and the cure are to be found within.

Be love.

Be light.

Be healing.

You shall find all these things radiating from within you and manifesting in your material world.

Moving Through the Lifestream

Beloved One, picture in your mind a magnificent waterfall that cascades over rocks until it moves into a clear, luminescent stream.

Watch the stream as it moves along its chosen pathway.

At its beginning, it is wide and powerful, and as it makes a surprise appearance from out of the trees, it cajoles you into joining in the music of its being, its existence.

Along the banks of the stream, nourished by water and sunshine, are many wildflowers and woodland trees.

In some places the water rushes forward with great speed.

In others, it eddies toward the banks and intermingles with the logs, rocks, and all aspects of its being.

It is one with all that it is.

And now, Beloved One, consider how the waters of the stream may be compared to human emotions—sometimes rushing or calm, other times frozen like the winter.

For many centuries we angels have observed how human emotions can be warm one moment—laughing musically like the sound of the stream—and at other times they can be blocked or frozen.

A stream never worries if a log or a large rock appears in its path. It finds ways around or over the block that has been suddenly imposed upon it.

Human emotion must also be expressed, then flow onward, like the fluid movement of the stream.

If the water truly becomes blocked, such as in the area around a beaver dam, it may become still and stagnant. And yet even in this condition there is a purpose and a lesson in the experience.

Emotions are forces of energy, such as that of the forward movement of the stream.

Find joy in the forward movement of your life-stream—for like the mountain stream, you have a purpose to fulfill that which is to be found within, in being and loving yourself.

Envision, Beloved One, a waterfall of light that constantly flows into your being.

Know within your heart that this waterfall of light from God is infinite, eternal.

Understand that there is no end to the waterfall of God's love that flows into your life experience and fills you from within.

Allow the constant flow of the waterfall of God's light, flowing from the heavens to you, to nourish you as the flow of the mountain stream nourishes the plant growth on its banks.

Allow God's heavenly messengers, the angels, to nourish your soul and to fill you with love.

Love attracts love.

Respect attracts respect.

Trust and faith attract trust and faith.

Invite the angels in to be a part of your lifestream, to be one with your conscious flow and guidance.

The Heavenly Gardens Where Angels Dance

Beloved One, know that we angels dance wherever love, beauty, truth, and light are present.

When this joyous dance occurs, those of Earth may detect the fragrance of roses. Such a divine fragrance is often produced when the angelic ones of wondrous, brilliant, intense frequencies are moved to a dance of celebration.

Thus, Beloved One, if you should detect the fragrance of roses when you are certain that no such physical flower is present, be aware that the angels are rejoicing—and allow the fragrance divine to bring feelings of joy and ecstasy to your soul.

Within the higher realms of heavenly light, there are gardens of roses, whose colors and beauty surpass that of the Earth experience.

These roses not only vibrate with love and joy in service to God, they emanate music. The heavenly roses share the light, the sound, the color, and the love vibration that comprises their existence.

The divine fragrance of a rose is a spiritual gift that is given to those on the Earth plane to uplift them into the soul remembrance of the etheric roses. Such a fragrance is a kind of reminder of the true, heavenly Home, and may thus bring tears of joy to human eyes.

I call such tears of happy release, "Showers of the Soul."

The fragrance of these divine roses is a gift that we angels bring to you as a gift of memory—a reminder that there is a God who loves you very much; that there is more than just a physical life; that you are beauteous, wondrous beings of love, light, wisdom, truth, and spiritual power.

We angels bring etheric rose petals of divinity all

around you to uplift the human heart and to make the soul soar with joy in the knowledge that God does dispatch heavenly messengers to watch over you.

Beloved One, you may envision many angels with dozens of roses in their arms, dancing all around you in luminescent sparkles of light and love.

When you chance to look upon the beauty of a rose garden in the early-morning hours, you often find drops of dew upon the soft, delicate petals. These drops of glistening dew are like pinpoints of wisdom in the quiet times of awareness.

Seek within the light that you are.

Feel within the love that you are.

Know within the truth that you are beings of pure love and pure light.

Recognize the reality of who you are and accept the gifts that God gives to you to share with others, for such gifts are for the higher good of all.

God's love is never for just one alone.

By Your Spiritual Fruits You Shall Be Known

Clearly flows forth the pure light of God to each individual being on Earth.

Clearly, purely, filled with intense, all-encompassing

love, the light of God flows forth to each heart engaged in the dance of life.

The wellspring of God's love is infinitely deep and without limit. It is a well of light that can provide you with the truth whenever you look within its depths during meditation.

The wellspring of God's love contains God consciousness, Angel consciousness, Love consciousness.

It also holds the consciousness of interconnectedness, the Oneness of all things.

This is the consciousness of respect for the sacredness of all life, from the ladybug crawling on a blade of grass to the eagle exploring the chartless skies.

It is the consciousness of knowing that there is spirit within all things.

You are the fruit of your own vine, the summation of all that you have been and have experienced on Earth.

Lift your thoughts, feelings, and actions high in intent and light.

Ask for our guidance in choosing always the right action, the pure thought, the proper emotion in all situations. We shall assist you in making your choices.

Let the fruits of your being be pure, sweet, and loving.

Let them provide spiritual nutrition, not only for your beloved self, but for others as well.

Let the fruits of your spirit be love; the fruits of your soul be compassion; the fruits of your heart be the intensity of God's light that shines forth.

You have often heard it said, "By their fruits, they shall be known." Test what you hear; test what you see and sense.

Be not like those three monkeys who cover eyes, ears, and mouths to avoid evil. Learn to discern truth by that which spirits speaks through the heart. Always test what you perceive—and the heart shall speak the truth.

By their fruits ye shall know them.

Listen for the truth that is unique to your own being.

Let your fruits radiate with divine fragrance, color, light, and the sweetness of love.

Be in the Present

Be in the present.

Bring the joy of the present moment into your life experience, then let go—and let God.

Does God not know each hair upon each being?

Does God not know your needs far in advance of your awareness?

Does God not see the overview from on high while you remain insecure of the path on ground level?

Meditate.

Pray.

Let go.

Let God—and you shall know that there is a God who loves you.

Angels of Light Hover Around You at All Times

Luminescent, sparkling, love-filled Angels of Light hover upon the airwaves and currents all around you at all times.

Beloved One, it matters not if you are aware of us or not, for according to the will of God—the Supreme All-That-Is and Creator of All—we move gently around you. We come as loving, light-filled energies that radiate and dance around your being, manifesting as colors, vibrations, frequencies, pulsating in harmony with the individual path that God hath set for your soul to travel.

Sometimes we may come with music in accordance with the highest forms of joyous harmonic tapestries, forming vibrational threads that interconnect all that is. We take great delight in bringing music that is in accordance with the God Light that dances beautifully around and about your soul and your physical body.

Such a magnificent rainbow waterfall of light flows always from the heavens above and within your heart.

We angels bring forth the harmonics of your lifestream, guiding you along your personal trail as you ascend to the higher realms.

Truly, I, Michael, advise you that what matters most is the journey, the ascending up the spiritual pathway. Take your time, Beloved One. Enjoy the view of your personal trail to the mountaintop.

We angelic beings bring you the love of God that is gentle, loving, transformative, all-encompassing, and all-knowing.

We gently hover about the harp strings of your heart, for we know your thoughts, as well as your words and deeds.

Nothing is hidden from us.

As we travel with you on your lifewalk, we bring with us a sparkling, silvery light.

You are never alone.

As we love, guide, and protect you, we wrap your soul essence in our own spiritual aura.

As you walk upward on the mountain path that is life on Earth, we help you so you do not stub your toe or walk off the edge.

We try our best to alert you to what you cannot see around the next bend, and we heal your very soul through the beauty of nature.

Most of all, we strive to lead you to the realization that you are one with God.

This is the way of the angelic ones.

You Are Spiritual Beings in Physical Bodies

Just out of the range of your sight, we angels hover, bringing you the power of God's love in each step you take.

Everywhere that you go, we go with you.

We hover well above the human notions of pettiness, prejudices, and ill-temper—all of which are illusion.

On occasion, we angels come around you and give you gentle hugs from behind, kisses upon the ear, and tousles of your hair.

Sometimes you may be able to see hints of our presence, for we often arrive with glorious sparkles of light or a luminescent glow that reflects the light of All-That-Is.

It is one of our greatest delights when we are able to inspire such love in your eyes and such a glow in your heart that your fellow beings can feel it deep within their own souls—even though you have not spoken a word.

Love that is pure, hath no words.

We come to you knowing the grander, more vast you.

We come to remind you of who you really are and to lift you up to join us in the dance of love—for love is the only dance there is.

We want you to love yourself and to see yourself as we do.

You are spiritual beings in physical bodies—not physical bodies searching for spiritual truth and meaning.

Know this truth! And know that you are one with God, the one who takes care of all things.

Have faith and trust your heart.

Revel in the miracle that you are on Earth, learning lessons and growing.

You have been given a rare opportunity at this time of evolution on the Earth plane.

Listen to your heart, not to the doom, gloom, or negativity of others.

Consciousness is rising on your planet.

Love will prevail.

Be at peace.

Surrender to the Springtime of the Soul

We angels are distressed when we behold the planet Earth and see that some souls are frozen like ice and are greatly in need of the warming rays of the Christ Light.

It is at such times that we strive to create new beginnings for such cold and closed human hearts and bring about the Springtime of the Soul and Heart. This new flow of energy melts the ice surrounding frigid hearts and brings about healing.

There is no cold, no ice, no hardness of heart, no pain, no sickness of the soul that cannot be healed by the warming rays of love brought into being by the Christ Light.

When the ice and snow in the Forest of Light and Life surrender to the Springtime of the Soul, the green grasses, flowers, and buds soon burst into new life centered within the Christ Light.

People of Earth Are Birthing into a New Era of Understanding

Beloved One, although you may not always perceive this truth from your evening news broadcasts or your newspapers, know that the wondrous pink rose of love is blooming fully over Earth and enveloping all of the planet in light.

The collective consciousness of many men and women and the combined light of thousands of spiritual seekers are awakening to a new era of understanding and light.

The Angelic Realms of Light, not always seen with the physical eyes, are being felt and sensed by millions throughout the world.

No one is untouched by the energy of the Christ Light. Of course all have freedom of choice as to how much of this vibration of love they will allow in their hearts, but many are freely permitting the golden candle flame of awareness within them to brighten.

As the Christ Light envelops the planet, each living entity is being touched on physical and etheric levels alike.

Some of the animals, birds, and sea creatures are actually progressing more quickly than some humans, for these entities do not resist the light or the love that it brings.

At this time there is a merger occurring between the Angelic Kingdom and the Divine Consciousness of Nature.

Many of the more sensitive humans are sensing the power of the angels within the forces of Nature and are responding with respect for all life. These enlightened people are acting with the motivation to protect—and not destroy—such areas as the rain forests in South America.

Many other inspired humans have responded to the plight of the dolphins, the whales, and other creatures of the sea, recognizing that they, too, are children of God.

Beloved One, know that all are interconnected and all are One.

In the etheric consciousness that exists within the light of the angelic realms, each nation of Earth possesses enormous potential to become fully realized as productive and spiritual people, consciously connected as One to the God Force.

All sentient entities, whether physical or unseen, are part of the process of oneness that we angels are assisting in facilitating.

It is like the birth of a wondrous infant. The loving mother suffers alone and experiences the pain of labor—but all may look upon the beauteous and precious result.

Let the truth of your being be made manifest through the light of your soul.

Let the Christ Light, the *I AM THAT I AM*, lift you above the illusions of humanity into the higher state of your own inherent divinity.

Such awareness is yours, patiently awaiting your recognition.

Come to the Infinite Temple of Truth

In the Angelic Realms there exists a wonderful place of love, wisdom, and light that we call the Infinite Temple of Truth.

The light of this wondrous place is available to all who desire to feel the ultimate truth of their being in the Christ Light.

In the Angelic Realms, the Temple is a real place wherein great teachers and teachings are available to spiritual seekers.

Seek the Temple in your meditations.

Ask and we shall assist you.

Ask and you shall receive.

CHAPTER FOUR

⌒

The Call of the
Angelic Kingdom

Beloved One, all around you in everyday life are the unseen mists of Angelic Light.

These mists of love and inspiration move amongst your every breath, word, thought, and deed.

Throughout all your waking and sleeping moments, we are there, knowing and hearing your thoughts, taking note of your emotions.

And always are we enfolding you in wondrous light.

I, Michael, tell you that we angels are ever-present, silently watching, ever-awaiting your invitation to become more a part of your life's events.

As the beauty of the snow silently falls in a forest, so doth the Christ Light come around you in gentleness and love in each moment.

And as each snowflake is unique and different, so are you humans honored for your individuality.

And as each snowflake issues from one Source, so doth each of you come from the One, the Creator, the Source of All-That-Is.

The Angelic Virtues

Among the angelic virtures are the following:

Love

Charity

Peace

Faith

Generosity

Humbleness

Gratitude

Kindness

Look within your heart, and you will find these same angelic attributes.

Be an ever-silent watcher for the flame of the Christ Light that dwells within the sacred sanctities of your heart and your soul.

Through the little extra efforts in the things that you do and the love you share, the flame within your heart grows ever brighter and more radiant.

And know this:

The brighter your aura becomes, the more your

light is noticed by those beings who shine with radiant illumination and love and who dwell in the Angelic Realms of Being.

Let Love Be Your Guide

Behold your unfoldment, Beloved One, as the very cells of your being become filled with the light of your true soul essence, rather than personality and ego—those aspects of your individuality that sometimes assert that the self is separate from and does not need the God Force. Such assertions are created from arrogance.

Release such thoughts and permit more beauty to fill your life as you center within the Christ Light.

Let love be your guide.

Permit yourself to unfold as graciously and as elegantly as wondrous angel wings.

Allow yourself to be nurtured by the God Force; and you, in turn, nurture the Creator through your loving, caring, sharing ways.

Permit your life to be fine-tuned by the Light, for you are an integral part of the symphony of life.

You are as a fine-tuned instrument, essential to create the music of harmony in the universal stream of light and life.

You Are Glorious in Your Totality

You are love. Beloved One, know that you humans are magnificent beings in your totality.

Accept this truth and be healed physically, mentally, spiritually.

You are beauteous beings of love, light, and gentle compassion.

You are spiritual, powerful beings of truth, love, and wisdom.

Your spiritual essence is truly so vast that all of the beauty of you cannot possibly fit into one mere physical body. Thus, you have a human body, an etheric body, an emotional body, a mental body, and a spiritual body.

All are a part of the light that you are in each moment that you experience. Thus, you are spiritual and physical multidimensional beings.

You are imbued with the purity of the Light that is God.

The totality of your light is grand, and your soul imbues the perfection of the Higher Realms.

As you are *on* the Earth plane, but not *of* it, allow your soul's light to become integrated with your everyday human activities and bless others with your love in the process.

I, Michael, ask you to attempt to see your world from the perspective of your soul.

Experience increased clarity and calm as you do this. The most profound things are usually found to be quite simple.

Do not attempt to force or to control.

Simply be.

You are glorious in your totality.

We are all a part of the Great I AM, the God Presence, the Light.

Give love.

Receive love.

Be love.

Be a Golden Star of Light

Look upward into the beauty and elegance of the night sky and see the wonder of yourself, sparkling with light.

Beloved One, you are a reflection of the magic of the stars, mirroring the light of God.

Envision yourself as one of those bright, golden stars of light that dance joyously in the sky each night.

Envision the limitless expanse of the universe.

See the angels dancing through the translucent beams of light that softly luminesce all that they touch.

Feel the aura of golden light that reaches out from within you.

See it moving ever outward, becoming a blessing to all that it touches.

See this magnitude of light within you as you walk upon the Earth plane.

Behold other beings touched with your light and your loving presence.

Be a golden star of light each day.

Let the light within your heart radiate outward to all that you see, feel, sense, and know.

Let your love and your kindness shine forth.

The Magic of Church Bells

Beloved One, consider the magic of church bells wherever they may be.

There is a clarity that rings through the air, clear and strong, true music to the ears as well as the soul.

When the sound of church bells is combined with the glories of nature anywhere upon the planet, an extra dimension of magic is added to the experience.

While listening to the bells peal, one may feel reverence, peace, beauty, and love. And you should definitely feel the energies of God's messengers, the angelic ones, bringing love to all.

Beloved One, you humans have the ability to lift

your consciousness while listening to the pealing of bells.

Know you, Beloved One, that in the Angelic Realms frequencies of light emit music, color, and harmony. With such energies of love, comes peace.

Listen to the sound of the bells of love ringing out to you from the God Force and reverberating within your heart. Listen within your being, and you will hear truth ringing out to you from your own soul.

Listen to the bells of light, calling to you and flowing forth with the love of the One, filling you and the planet with healing.

THE CELESTIAL BRIDGE THAT REACHES TO EARTH FROM HEAVENLY REALMS

Beloved One, you know that there are many kinds of bridges on Earth. Some kinds of bridges are seen with the physical eyes, others are not.

Life is filled with bridges, material and spiritual.

In your physical world, a bridge is something that takes you from one side of a river, canyon, brook, and so forth, to the other. In either its physical or ethereal embodiment, a bridge is an instrument of transition.

Some bridges are old, like certain beliefs and pre-conceptions within your societies on Earth. Such bridges thus require discernment before crossing.

Some of these antiquated bridges, regardless of how solidly they may have been built, should be dismantled and reconstructed to make way for newer and stronger structures.

Reflect for a moment upon the word "bridge" and what it brings to your knowing.

From the mental level of knowing, a bridge is a journey from one point of consciousness to another. Life is filled with quantum leaps that are part of new growth, new consciousness.

From the knowing of the heart, the journey to higher awareness is found within the God Light.

Listen to your heart to see what bridge to new awareness resonates best with your inner knowing.

Always test within to determine what feels right for you and what does not.

Each bridge that is crossed—be it etheric or physical—is a step upon the lifestream, the journey of the heart and soul upon planet Earth.

Which bridges are filled with loving light and which are not?

There are many bridges to cross upon the path of your lifestream, Beloved One. Remember, as I have said before, truly, growth is attained during the journey and not at the destination.

Change will be a constant in your life.

Growth is optional.

The daily bridge between the God Light and the heart within brings pearls of wisdom.

Wisdom enables the soul to perceive the material world more clearly and to see how the pebble of love that has been placed into the pool of your awareness is able to create ripples that reach out to others.

Each time a baby is born on Earth, its soul has crossed from the celestial bridge of heaven to the physical world.

Each time one makes the transition known as death, the soul crosses a bridge to a different side of reality and experience.

The journey proceeds eternally, for there is infinity to experience. There is more light and love to know.

Know, Beloved One, that you are as safe as your thoughts.

Your inner God Light and the presence of angels will carry you across all the celestial bridges that span the etheric worlds.

We angels are ever watching over each footstep that you take, each breath of air that you inhale and exhale.

Truly, we are closer to you than your own heartbeat.

Know, Beloved One, that when you think of us angels, we are there.

You are never alone.

Never.

Through all of time, we cross back and forth on the celestial bridge that stretches from Earth to the Angelic Realms.

The Marvel of a Seashell

As I have said, Beloved One, the Angelic Realms exist on many levels; and when the angels visit Earth, they may not always be seen, but their love energy may always be felt as you gaze into the beauty of nature.

Perhaps you have seen a sunset that seemed so beautiful that you pretended that God had painted it just for you.

I am certain that you felt the love and awe within your heart as you drank in the splendor of that sunset. Quite likely your soul was filled and soothed by the loveliness of the colors arrayed before you.

The place where ocean waters touch the sands of the beach is a special place of magic and love that vibrates to its own energy and pulse.

See in your mind a number of seashells scattered at the water's edge.

Each shell upon the beach is unique.

Each has its own story, its own journey of evolution.

Each carries the special energies of its own experience.

Visualize yourself picking up a seashell to feel its particular energy.

Try to imagine where it has been.

Notice the intricacy, the delicate beauty of the shell.

Observe how this particular shell is different from the others and has its own unique way of being.

Consider the ways in which you are like a seashell.

Reflect upon the different sizes and shapes of human beings.

Think of how people have their own intricacies and individuality.

From the soul level, you designed how you came into the world prior to your birth.

On the soul level, you knew what lifepath you most needed to fulfill your own lessons and spiritual growth.

Like the individual seashell, you are beautiful and special.

You have your very own story to tell.

Your particular history is unlike that of anyone else, yet within God's love, *all are one.*

So it is even with the many grains of sand that make up the beach.

Each grain is unique, yet the beach could not exist without the oneness of the millions of grains of sand.

Think for a moment of each grain of sand as a single human being—and then the entire beach as humanity together.

Each is essential.

Each is necessary.

In the mind of God, there is no separatism of race, culture, creed, or appearance.

So, too, must you understand that all humans are of the one heart and all have lessons to learn from one another.

Truly, it is as if the same heart beats within each chest; and the heart within knows not color or creed. It simply knows that it has life and love to impart.

Come home to the Oneness and the love of God for you.

The Love Force Increases the Consciousness of Earth

As surely as the Light of God comes forth to bless the inner light of each soul, the angels offer humankind an ever-present source of courage, strength, awareness, trust, and love.

Charity is very near for each heart that asks for angelic assistance in those matters that strife for the highest good of all.

In these present times of stress, strife, and discordant energies, God's love is increasing the consciousness of Earth.

The Love Force is coming forth like a bright chariot of light brought by white horses of compassion.

Answered prayers are speeding ever forth from the heavens to Earth.

The path of selfless service that the angels tread is dedicated to the raising of human consciousness.

Ask for the highest good of all, and you shall receive.

Spiritual Awareness Requires Everyday Effort

As you walk your "mountain path" of life, be aware of all things around you and how each one relates to your spiritual growth.

Sometimes your path may be straight, smooth, and level.

Other times there will be uphill zigs and zags and sharp downhill turns.

Become aware of the mirrors that the Universe puts in place along your lifepath so that you may monitor your growth.

Take time to breathe deeply and to notice the little things along the path.

Notice the textures and colors of life all around you.

Set aside time to rest, to take a break.

Don't rush through life.

Spiritual awareness is an everyday process, not a grand race to some cosmic finish line.

Prepare for the uphill climbs on your lifepath, but always take a moment to pause and look around you even in the midst of trudging upward.

And once at the top of the ridge, congratulate your heart on its accomplishment and take time to breathe the clean air, to feel the breeze in your face, and to look around you at the new view.

It will soon be time enough to start off for the next high ridge.

As the winds of change blow around you, ask the Angelic Realms for assistance—and you shall be safely guided. God will always send an angel to assist you if you ask with sincerity.

Fear not.

To think that any force other than God is in control would be illusion.

The God Light within knows the way along the most difficult paths of life and through the roughest terrains that might be encountered.

Worry not.

Wherever you journey, an angelic being is always there to walk beside you, to hold your hand, to carry you if necessary.

Be blessed within this knowing.

The Wondrous Light of God Illuminates Your Every Step

Precious Child, during the course of life's journey there are many levels of consciousness from the Angelic Realms that call out to you for greater awakening, awareness, and learning.

You may find access to the wondrous Light of God that can illuminate your every step by entering the great silence of meditation. Your journey through your inner world can lead your way through the outer world.

Meditate—and receive a clearer view of the celestial blueprint that God has drafted for you.

Let go of the material world, enter the great silence, and a key shall be given to you that will enable you to open even more doors through meditation and the power of prayer.

Beloved Dove of my heart, know you that growth takes place in integrated steps that become more and more refined, more and more brilliant, like a diamond that has been polished on all of its facets.

As you awaken more to the Light, to the interconnectedness of all things, to the Oneness within your own heart, yet another layer of your consciousness is peeled away and more light and awareness is revealed.

Know always that we of the Angelic Realms are here, waiting to enfold you in love, protection, and guidance.

Unseen friends are always near you.

When you call upon us, we are there.

When you think of us, we are there.

You are never alone.

Child of Light, I take you in my arms and hold you close to my heart and the heart of God.

Know that God is in control of all things.

There is truly no other controlling force than the loving, compassionate, Divine Will of God, which wishes only to infuse your soul with joy, light, healing, and love.

Allow your soul to be infused with Divine Light and Love, whose purity hath no words.

CHAPTER FIVE

The Sanctity of the Soul

The soul is God's divine expression mirrored through individual and collective humanity and tended by the angels as if it were a work of the finest art.

Beloved One, the soul is the heart-centered connection between the human and the divine. Each soul is a part of the magnificent I AM.

There is an interconnectedness that exists within all people and subtly extends to all animals and all of creation on Earth, including the elements of earth, wind, water, and fire.

The Christ Light is all encompassing; thus to center within the light that is truly you is to center within the All-That-Is, God.

You are your soul.

Your soul is you.

You are an elegant expression of God's love and grace.

Like the warming rays of the Sun on a cold, winter day, centering in the Christ Light brings a glow to your soul and manifests healing to the mental and emotional aspects of self.

Behold the Light of Your Soul in All of Nature

Look around you and see the reflection of your soul's light in all of the beautiful works of nature. The wondrous divinity of yourself is seen in the multihued mirrors that nature holds for your self-examination.

With the new awareness created by your centering in the Christ Light, you reach a level of knowing that tells you that nature is sacred and that all humankind shares responsibility for being loving caretakers of Earth.

All of the members of God's family are one. It matters not what facet of creation is expressed, from the lowliest insect to the full expression of humanity.

Behold the Soul Light in Your Fellow Humans

When you smile at your fellow human beings and bless them, be aware of the Soul Light to be seen behind the eyes of each person you meet.

Each human soul needs love. All else is illusion.

Within the Christ Light flowing through the soul there exists a seed of light. This ever-bright white and golden spark never goes out. It is always present.

This spark of light is present in varying degrees in the soul light of the many. Just as candle flames burn to varying intensities, so does the Christ Light shine brighter in some human hearts than other.

But the flame of God never dies out, no matter how long it may have to sputter in some hardened hearts until certain stubborn individuals gain the awareness that they, too, are a part of God and have the ability to center with the Christ Light.

When you are centered within the Christ Light, you cannot help smiling brightly in divine blessing to all whom you meet.

Each Facet of Light Is Different

Allow your intention to say that you are willing to open to the wonders of the Light within your heart and soul.

Simply relax—and be!

Each mode of expression is individual. There is no one way to God, no *one* truth. Many roads lead to the temple within.

In your meditations, simply relax and be.

There are limitless ways to meditate, from walking in the woods to mowing the lawn to sitting in your living room.

The light in you is limitless.

God is limitless.

All beings of light, including the beauteous angels, are limitless.

Tumble Walls and Open Hearts with the Christ Light

When you center within the Christ Light, walls come tumbling down and hearts open. Your energy radiance shifts and through your acts of love and kindness, others can arrive at shifts in their own growth as well.

Truly, the simplest things can become the most profound. A smile is a beautiful gift of the soul—an expression of light that shines through the eyes and the total being.

The Pink Light of Love

Beloved One, beauteous, soft pink is the color, the vibrational frequency, ever-flowing through the heart of love.

Love is the divine light—the light of a million expressions.

Love is the gift that brings miracles, large and small.

Miracles are the natural expression of the light of the divine that dances around you—healing, rejuvenating, and bringing joy to other hearts.

The light of love is truly the most powerful force that exists—and Beloved One, you are a physical expression of the light of love.

Visualize the color of pink as if it were a blanket of love that comes to soothe you, to give comfort to your heart and soul.

Allow the love of the Christ Light to smile through your heart and to radiate through your eyes, your smile, your aura, to each one you meet.

Look at the light of the soul that shines behind and through the eyes of each person you encounter on the path of life.

Each human being is an expression of the light that encompasses the Family of God—of which we are all One.

Visualize the color of pink and permit it to fill each cell of your body, flowing, cleansing, healing, and uplifting—until you are like a fountain of pink love light overflowing.

Be love.

Give love.

Live love.

Express love.

That is all that matters.

The One God Force Sustains All Souls

Beloved One, I, Michael, bring you my purest light and love.

When you are centered within the Christ Light, the Oneness of all things becomes evident within all levels of your being.

No longer is there a sense of separation with any other level of life—be it within the inner or the outer levels of your perceived reality. All perceived levels of separation that emanate in daily life from the outer appearances of others simply fall away.

When you are centered within the Christ Light, it shall no longer make any difference what color or culture another person may be. No longer shall it matter how others may choose to express their individual reality.

The one God Force sustains all souls, all beings. There is something to learn from each person, whether black, white, brown, red, or yellow.

Forgive others.

Bless them.

Each being has a pathway, a blueprint, that only God knoweth.

Your responsibility as an individual soul is to be the best that you can be upon your own pathway.

Judge not others, for only All-That-Is knows the reasons for each entity's life experiences.

When you are centered within the Christ Light, you will see clearly the need to permit others to be who they are and how they are.

Again I tell you—only the God Force knows the reasons for the course of each lifestream.

The Sacred Essence of Each Soul Is a Part of the Great Mystery of Life

Beloved One, you are pure light and pure love. You are one with the moon and the stars, as well as the lowliest of creatures. But you are a powerful *spiritual being* much more than you are a *physical entity*.

Beloved One, there are many secrets and mysteries to life and to the universe.

There are truths that have always been present and that continue to be discovered and forgotten—then rediscovered once again.

You are a part of the Great Mystery that is called life. This hidden aspect of yourself is an element of the magic and beauty of your own soul being.

When you are silent in meditation and centering

within the Christ Light, many new doors to the mystery of your own soul growth shall be opened to you.

We angels can lead you to the "light switch," so to speak, but, ultimately, it is you alone who must reach forward and turn on the light of new awareness.

Each step of the way, you are guided and loved.

In meditation, allow your being to be filled with the purity, serenity, and peace from which all-knowing comes.

All answers are within.

The sacred essence of your being is within.

The way home to Heaven is illuminated by the light within your own soul.

Exercise Your Spiritual Muscles

Beloved One, consider an example from the truth that lies in nature.

When the small, newborn fawn first tries to get up on its spindly and awkward legs soon after birth, it finds the task difficult at best. It is still wet from its mother's tongue, and it tries again and again to rise on its thin, wobbly legs.

The fawn falls and falls again, finally perceiving that its new legs are not quite yet strong enough to support it. So the fawn rests, then tries again until success is achieved.

Gingerly, the fawn takes one small step at a time until it is confident to walk without falling.

Before long, the small, determined creature is able to run and to play in all assurance that those once wobbly legs will now take it wherever it desires to go.

The fawn soon ventures out of the forest shadows and experiences the direct rays of sunshine for the first time in its young life. The sunlight warms the tiny deer and makes it feel good.

And through all these first forays into life, the mother doe has been keeping a close eye on the fawn, ever-protective and loving, ever-ready to nurture, guide, and teach the young deer.

Beloved One, you, too, have spiritual legs and muscles to stretch and to exercise. You need to discover these muscles and learn how best to use them in the forest of life.

Through the process of centering within the Christ Light, you will learn that there are many new discoveries to be made, new spiritual muscles to develop, new strength to be gained.

And the Source, the God Force, is always present, ever-nurturing, guiding, loving, and protecting you, just as the mother doe does with her fawn.

The fawn trusts that its mother doe will protect it and care for it, so that it may play in the forests, knowing that its needs will be provided.

So it is with the God Force, who has sent angels to protect the sanctity of your soul and to provide you with unconditional love.

CHAPTER SIX

❧

The Purity of the Higher Realms

Beloved One, when you have truly meditated and entered the great inner silence to perceive the pure energies of the God Force, you will understand that it is up to you as to how you will choose to qualify these energies within your thoughts, emotions, and actions.

Those who are meek, gentle, and humble of heart shall truly know the purity of the Kingdom of Heaven within.

To be truly humble is to know that although you are a cocreative partner with the God Force, it is the Light moving through you—and not you—that is the essence of All-That-Is.

Be an instrument of love in your everyday activities. Understand that it is the heaven within you that has recognition of the Heaven above.

As above, so below.

Open Your Spiritual Wings

As you open your spiritual wings, you soar high in consciousness and enter etheric frequencies and vibrations that will draw you to new avenues of experience.

As the God Force supports the angels, the Light Beings, so, too, will you be nurtured by All-That-Is in your spiritual growth.

You will be given strength to soar ever higher as you discover, uncover, and rediscover the magnificent elegance of the God Light within the heart that sustains all.

Listen to your heart within. This is where God speaks quietly and gently with you.

Listen to the silence within, and you shall hear much.

Feel the Higher Frequencies of Light in Your Heart

The higher, intense frequencies of the vibration that is the Christ Light may not always be seen with the physical vision. However, as you increase your level of spiritual God Consciousness, you will not only perceive the Light with your eyes, but you will feel it through your heart.

Always is the Light of the Christ felt through the heart, for the Light of Oneness is love.

Beloved One, care for one another, love one another, for love is all that matters.

Love is the greatest gift that exists.

Earth Is the Divine Jewel of Love

Love is the divine fragrance from which all existence finds birth, creation, imagination, and inspiration to express and to share.

Beloved One, you are an expression of Divine Love, and you must share it with your fellow human beings and all other living entities on the planet.

Earth is the divine jewel of love. Respect her and know that you are part of the consciousness of the planet and she is a part of the consciousness of each being residing upon her.

All is as one in God's Light.

Inspiration Is a Divine Gift from God

To be inspired is a divine gift from God that we angelic beings bring forth to nudge you gently as we walk beside you and guide you to the complete knowing that you are one with God.

Inspiration brings about the understanding that all sisters and brothers on Earth are one within God's love. Truly, this is a most luminescent gift.

Seek the truth within, and you shall feel the light.

The Violet Light of God

Beloved One, the fragrance, the light, the color of violet fills the air.

The essence of violet moves along on the breeze of light over your lifestream, dancing and bringing joy.

You may know well the beauty and the fragrance of lavender and lilacs.

It is a fragrance that uplifts and transmutes emotions, feelings, and consciousness.

It is a fragrance that permits you to relax and to allow God's peace to fill your entire being.

The Violet Light of God flows through the unseen world, transmuting, uplifting, purifying, and clarifying. It brings discordent energies back to their source to be cleansed.

Call upon the beauteous gift of the color of violet to flow through your every life experience.

The Violet Flame, the spiritual light of the One, comes to each being as pure energy.

It is up to each entity to qualify the light of God through one's thoughts, words, and actions—and to keep them high.

Be conscious of how your choices in life may affect others.

Human actions may often express the ripple effect of the pebble in the pond. Radiate love, so that it is love that your actions shall ripple out to others.

The Rainbow Luminescence that Streams from Heaven

The rainbow luminescence and the elegant grace of God's Light streams and flows from the heavens to enter each heart and to bring forth the intensities of the extreme frequencies of light and love.

The sound ray and the translucent light ray, both on the etheric level, bring forth the purity that is above all third-dimensional expression and experience. These combine to form the pure, golden radiation of God within and about all things.

Like infinity and the never-beginning and never-ending of Alpha and Omega, the rainbow luminescence from the heavens form a constant circle of love.

The rainbow light of All-That-Is envelops many paths and truths and exists in all light beings and in all people. Within this heavenly rainbow of light, all colors come together in balanced and beauteous harmony, thus blending into a love for one another.

The rainbow luminescence that flows from the heavens to Earth, encompasses and covers all, like a cloak of translucent radiance that touches all receptive hearts.

Within the light of the rainbow from the heavens only love exists.

To be within the rainbow luminescence is to live only with compassion and respect for others.

The rainbow luminescence fills the outer and inner levels of Earth reality with a joy that causes the heart to dance and to join in a magnificent chorus of celebration.

Each soul upon the planet and within the heavens is a member of a marvelous rainbow symphony that vibrates in praise of the One.

Allow this rainbow of heavenly light to break through the gray storm clouds in your life.

Be still and know that this rainbow of grace, faith, and love completely envelops the entire planet, and be aware that it is filled with angels who come as messengers of love.

In your meditations, envision the angel-filled rainbow of luminescence flowing from the heavens.

Allow the Light of God to encompass your heart with love and with your own special truth.

Know that you are a being of pure light and pure love who has come to Earth to serve with gentleness and loving example.

Worry not if your actions are not always understood by others who may not perceive the true source of your love.

Simply teach with the example of love and know that truth will touch the hearts of those who are ready to receive the Christ Light.

The White Cross of Christ Light that Shines Upon the Planet

Beloved One, never think that we angels do not watch over you. Paradise is once again being found— one heart at a time.

Envision a cross of white light within the planet that radiates to all ends of Earth. The same white Christ Light flows forth with love to move through all the hearts upon Earth that are willing to behold its magnificence.

More and more, the ribbons of love and of the brilliant frequency of white Christ Light are moving forth to bless each and every heart upon the planet— and throughout the entire universe.

Know you this: Each one of you is precious. Each one of you is essential. The complete integration of

God's intent to bring forth a renewed paradise on planet Earth cannot be completed without each and every one of you.

There is not one upon the planet who is better or less than another. To think otherwise is to entertain arrogance and illusion. Each soul is precious in the eyes of God.

What we angels wish most is that you humans fill your hearts with the knowledge and the awareness that you are all on the way home to God-awareness and the divine light within. Listen, listen to the wisdom within as it speaks to you.

As each of you joins hands with another with compassion and love upon the precious planet, Earth shall be transformed into the world of love that she was always meant to be.

Simply teach with the example of love and know that truth will touch the hearts of those who are ready to receive the Christ Light.

Multicolored Ribbons of Light Shimmer to Earth

There are bands of sparkling energy that flow like multicolored ribbons of light from the heavens to each heart upon Earth. In like manner, there are many millions of bright, luminescent and opalescent ribbons of love, faith, and light that issue forth from the precious, beloved ones of Earth to the heavens above. It is a beauteous, wondrous sight to behold these ribbons of light, shimmering and shining like mother of pearl.

Beloved One, heaven exists within your heart, and blooms therein like a delicate rose. The light of God's infinity and divinity intertwines within each shimmering ribbon and touches the gentle rose petals of each heart.

Envision a pole of white light entwined with hundreds of long ribbons of every color, flowing freely, gracefully in the breeze of God's expression.

Envision the way in which these ribbons of love move purposefully in the same direction as the gentle breezes blow.

All ribbons are connected to the same pole of white light, the same light that reaches upward to the heavens, yet connects on Earth within each heart.

Come and join the dance of love and of light. It is a wondrous, divine dance, my Beloved Child of the One. It is within this dance that your pure essence exists.

The ribbons flow unhindered and untangled. They flow individually and yet as one.

The pole of God's white light is solid and cannot be damaged. Neither can the ribbons be torn or tangled in purpose when they are all interconnected and one with God and his light—*your* light.

Share this light of oneness with each other in compassion and in love. Don't fall back into old positions of rigidity. Throw your blinders away.

Care for the jewel of Earth upon which you reside. Love her, and she will love you, as she always has. Allow the heart of Earth and all the creation upon her to flow freely.

Join the dance of love and joy. Celebrate the brilliant magnificence that is your soul.

Join the ribbon of your being with all the other ribbons on the pole of white light—the same light that illuminates the heavens within your heart and touches all others throughout the cosmos.

Let the illumination of your soul light shine upon the vastness of your being that is so very much more than you see in your mirror.

Let the multitude of ribbons that flow from the tall pole of God's white love and light become as one ribbon of brilliant luminescence, fully integrated with the Light of All-That-Is.

Join us angels in our song of joy as we sparkle and shine with the warmth of love within. *So be it!*

CHAPTER SEVEN

Be Uplifted from Everyday Strife

Archangel Michael Shares a Meditative Exercise

Beloved One, I will tell you how best to prepare for this meditative exercise for centering yourself within the Christ Light.

For purposes of this meditation, it is best to be sitting in an upright position. If it is more comfortable for you to lie down, that is also all right.

Know that while you are doing this exercise you shall have the full support of the angels. I am also available to assist you upon your request.

Create a quiet space for yourself in a place and time when you will not be interrupted.

It is important to create a special sacred space for yourself in which you will be totally comfortable and in which you will feel nurtured and loved.

Know that the angels will share with you the joy and the magic of your special place, for it is a place where they may assist you and commune together with you.

You might choose to have a candle burning or the fragrance of incense in the air.

You might wish to play some soothing and re-laxing music to help create an atmosphere of peace, tranquillity, and love.

The important thing is that you are able to relax completely and totally.

Just be in the present moment and allow all else to fall away from you.

Be certain to make your physical embodiment as comfortable as possible with pillows or whatever, so that you will be able to relax and let go.

If there should be troublesome thoughts on your mind, you might want to jot them down so that they may be released until later when you are able to return to them at a more convenient time.

It is important *just to be.*

Allow your mind and your physical being to be quiet and at peace.

Release all anticipations and expectations of what you think might occur during this experience.

When you allow yourself to let go and let God with trust, you will find that you will receive so much more than you may have expected.

It is when you enter the silence within that heaven is found in your heart.

The angels will be assisting you every moment. Accept their aid with childlike innocence and love, for it is when one is as a child that heaven is found within.

Begin the process of the meditative exercise by becoming aware of your breath as it moves in and out of your physical being.

Breathe slowly, long and deep.

Inhale through your nose.

Continue to breathe in until it feels as though your lungs have no more space for air to be inhaled. Then allow your breath to be slowly exhaled through the mouth.

Many in the physical world have not learned to breathe properly, and their bodies do not receive enough oxygen. Allow yourself to practice this slow, relaxed, deep breathing process until you feel a comfortable rhythm. You will begin to find yourself feeling quieter, calmer, and more relaxed.

If you should begin to feel a bit light-headed while

attaining a comfortable rhythm to your breathing, simply let go and proceed slowly.

You shall remain in a conscious state during this exercise. You may come to feel sensations within your physical embodiment that you have not previously experienced in such ways, such as a warmth, a tingling, colors behind the eyelids.

All these sensations are natural and individual.

There is no right or wrong way to perform this exercise. Each individual way is the right way.

When you have allowed yourself a few minutes to breathe slowly, deeply, in and out, a sense of calm will be felt. You will experience a sense of having slowed down, which will enable you to listen quietly within.

Now, in your mind's eye, your imagination, visualize a beautiful golden flame.

If you cannot see it at first, simply *know* and *feel* that a beautiful golden flame is there.

It is as if you are sitting in the center of a candle flame of light.

This is not a physical flame that might burn you. This is a flame made of sparkling light filled with warmth and love.

It is what we angels would term a "spiritual fire."

Allow yourself to linger in this wondrous light and to feel its warmth and its love.

It is the Light of God moving around you, enveloping you—below, on each side, within.

Know that this light is connected to your heart.

Feel now a great transmutation of any concerns that you may have in your life.

This is your special time—a time of being able to feel calm, loved, and safe.

Now within this wondrous light, envision that you are like a pearlescent rose that is unfolding and blooming.

Each petal of this rose represents a beautiful aspect of yourself.

The fragrance of the rose is your spiritual essence, wafting through the breezes of your life, blessing others.

Within the center of the rose is your own beautiful face, filled with love.

There is now a wondrous light that is flowing to you from above, and it is pouring into the top of your head.

It flows into your physical embodiment until every cell of your body is filled with beautiful white light from above.

This light is one that balances, refreshes, heals, and loves you.

See now that the White and Golden Lights are

blended together into one as the Christ Light, the loving light of God.

Listen within your heart to the voice of divinity saying that you are a precious child of God.

You are a part of the God Force, just as the God Force is a part of you.

Allow yourself to remain in this peaceful place and, passively, observe or listen to whatever feeling may come to you.

You will feel the love of God within yourself.

When you have completed this meditation, you will be filled with peace and love—and you will take these feelings with you wherever you go or whatever you do.

At any time during your day or night, you may say to yourself, "I am of the Light. I am surrounded by Light."

Immediately, you will once again experience the peace and love of this spiritual process.

God Is Alive in All Things

Beloved One, do you know of the Canadian snow geese that navigate the currents of air in their flight high above the lands below?

They fly together as a team in the shape of a great

V. Observe how in their flight they express confidence, elegance, and grace.

There is a lead goose that flies at the point of the V, no doubt working harder in flight, so those flying behind have an easier path to follow.

As with all of God's children of light, be they human, animal, or bird, the geese are special as well.

You ask what this has to do with my teachings of wisdom and of light? I shall tell you.

Lift your consciousness high into the upper levels of awareness as the geese soar high into the upper currents of air. They rely upon their inner knowingness, not asking why.

They simply *know* and do.

Lift your consciousness into the higher realms and see life more clearly.

With simple faith and trust, know that all of your needs will be met.

Follow the voice of God as the winged ones follow the call of the lead goose.

Beloved One, remember that God is alive in all things.

The God Force sustains all, whether the smallest forest creatures that rustle the fallen leaves or the great birds above them that part the higher currents of air as they migrate.

Listen to the Voice of Your Soul

Beloved One, I, Michael, beseech you to reach high to the heights of your beauteous consciousness of light. Reach deep into the depths of your heart and listen to the voice of your soul.

The voice of your soul comes as gently as the fluttering of angel wings and is as deep as all-encompassing love.

If only you will silence the mind in meditation, you will hear, feel, and know the purity of God's love for you.

Within your periods of meditation and silence, join the joy of the multitudes of the Angelic Host who dance in the unseen airwaves around you.

The Sacred Places of Earth

Beloved One, know that there are sacred places upon your planet.

There are places of great spiritual vibration, such as Machu Picchu, the pyramids of Egypt, Mount Sinai.

There are many more sacred power places that are as yet unknown to humankind. These places are now buried deep within the Earth, and they relate to civilizations past that are undiscovered and unknown to present-day humankind.

These civilizations are not to be found in the history books. Some lay under present-day oceans, and some are buried deep within the South American continent.

Some day in the future, when humankind comes together fully within the love of the One, these ancient civilizations will be revealed unto them.

Within these long-ago places existed the natural knowing that all are one with God, and life was lived in accordance with its universal truth.

We angels seek always for all humans to know that God is one with you and that you are one with God.

Be aware that when you have this knowing within your heart and entertain no further doubts of its truth, then the very ground upon which you stand becomes a place of spiritual power. Your awareness and knowing have created a power place, a sacred spot.

Each child of God is a chosen one. Bring this knowing within your hearts as you move through your day and you shall find small miracles and blessings that you have previously overlooked.

Most of all, you will discover the miracle that is you.

Love Deeply and Fear Not

Picture in your mind an infant child, newly born and pink.

Visualize this expression of its own soul light through the radiance and the love that is God.

Each human being is a child of God.

Allow yourself to be as vulnerable as a newborn babe.

The God Force shall care for you.

Release your concerns, and all shall be given to you.

The Light of God comes to each soul, pure and unadulterated.

It is up to each individual to determine how that light shall be qualified through words, thoughts, and actions.

The God Light has within its force field all expression that exists in all realms, in all places. There can be nothing but love within All-That-Is.

Judgment exists only within the realm of Earth.

Judgment is not of God.

Within each soul is the capacity to make of life a heaven or a hell for itself.

When the physical body passes into the state known as death, each soul entity examines the life it has just lived and perceives an evaluation of gain or loss.

Live your life to the fullest.

Be compassionate.

Love deeply and fear not.

When your time comes to leave the physical body and be evaluated for passage into the higher realms, the questions presented to you may be the following:

How well and how deeply did you love?

How much compassion did you show to others of the human expression?

At no time will you be asked how many material possessions you acquired or how many physical activities you mastered.

There Must Be Love of Self Before It Is Given to Others

Beloved One, show love; feel love; be love; share love.

Know that you are the divine human expression of a love that is so vast that it is beyond finite comprehension in its totality.

All troubles perceived on Earth emanate from two things—fear and a lack of love for self and for others.

The perfect energies of the God Force come to you first from within the depths of your own spirit. You must realize the expression of the God Force as love of self before you can express its energies toward others.

Truly, all good that is perceived in others exists

also within your wondrous self. This must be so, or you would not be able to recognize it!

Seek the Light of the Christ first within yourself, then share the gifts of its love with others—for love is always meant to be shared.

When you see the spark of Christ Light in others, you recognize it within the expression of the soul and the heart.

You see it in people's eyes, in their smiles, in the light that radiates from their auras.

You see it in the very inner being of others on the path to the higher realms.

Within your meditations, energetically radiate love to others. Send it along with your positive thoughts from your heart.

Feel the gifts of the Christ Light—love, humility, creativity, inspiration.

Be aware that all blessings come first from the spiritual realms and then to you, not *vice versa*.

Most importantly, love and fear not.

When another asks you, "How can I ever thank you?" reply thusly: "Just take the love that I give you and pass it on to someone else. That's all you need to do."

Share your smile—and know that if everyone were to show one other person love, your planet would soon be the paradise of light that it was truly meant to be.

The Dance of Love and Light that Encompasses All of Earth

Beloved One, I, Michael, invite you to come with me and join the dance of love and light!

The dance of lights swirls to the higher levels of love, light, and freedom.

The dance of love blends with the higher frequencies of light that issue forth from the heart of the Creator.

The bells of freedom ring forth within each heart, as the dance of love comes to Earth to bring her blessed residents home to the awareness that all are one.

It is the softness of the dance of love that opens, enlightens, and brings gentleness to each heart to share.

Love one another.

Treasure one another.

Share with one another.

Assist one another with love and without thought of return, control, or obligation.

Give love simply for the sake of giving—not with the thought of what you will receive in return.

Paradise can be created with one beloved soul at a time.

Beloved One, do not feel as though you personally are not doing enough, for if you have touched and uplifted even one heart, it is known in the heavens. Each heart is beloved to God.

The dance of light swirls ever more, encompassing Earth and all of her beloved ones.

The dance of light and love encapsulates a radiance more brilliant than any luminescence that you have seen thus far.

Join the dance of love, Beloved One. Accept the love of the heavens in your heart—then share it with other hearts.

A Lesson of Caves and Wolves

Beloved One, know that the wolf and the cave that it may claim as its home are as much a part of the Oneness as each human, bug, bird, or any other expression of God's love.

Throughout all of human time caves have held mysteries and new awarenesses to be discovered.

Pause for a moment and envision a cave in which a mother wolf has given the miracle of birth into the new physical expression of many pups. For a time, these innocent babes are dependent upon their mother for all things, for protection, for warmth, and for nourishment in the cool darkness of their cave.

Consider that as they grow and begin to open their eyes, they become curious of what lies beyond the boundary of the cave entrance. They can glimpse sunshine, green grasses, and a new and different world for themselves.

As the mother wolf continues to care for them, the day arrives when they first venture outward into the sunshine. At the same time, they yet enjoy the innocence and joy of puppyhood, for their mother still provides for all their needs.

Once those pups have journeyed forth from the darkness of their cave and have experienced the outer world of the sun, they will never again be contented to remain within the cold shadows of stone.

So it is that once you have begun to gain awareness, once you have ventured forth into the light, you will never again be the same.

You cannot reside in darkness, then venture into the light and not forever remember the experience.

Neither can one forget love.

The gift of love must be shared, just as that mother wolf unselfishly shared her love to her pups.

Beloved One, what we angels seek to teach you is that God's light and God's love is constant.

When you sometimes feel as though you are surrounded by darkness or lost in a cave during the course of your lifepath, know that you can always step into the light. You always have the ability to center yourself, let go, and let the Light of God surround you.

Allow the Light of God to provide for your needs and to nurture you with spiritual energy and love.

Pearls of Wisdom

Within the oyster cometh a divine treasure of immense beauty, purity, and light. The pearl is an illumined gift from nature.

The beauteous pearl is produced through an irritation within the shell of the oyster.

In the same way, Beloved Child of Light, through refinement of character the love of the Creator grows within your heart as a pearl of wisdom.

Just as the oyster produces the brilliant, gentle white radiance of a pearl after the passing of time, so is it with your growing awareness and soul beauty.

Pearls of wisdom are of the purest, most intense frequencies of Light. They are gifts from God to be shared with others.

Know well, Blessed Child, that you are a pearl of indescribable beauty and radiance in God's eyes.

Seek within the silence of your hearts during your meditations and ye shall find pearls of wisdom.

Seek within the light that you are and that with which the angels of God are eager to bless you.

Seek within the love that you are and discover that the completion that you desire exists already within your heart.

Seek within the truth that you are and know that you are pure love and pure light.

As a pearl grows within an oyster, so does your awareness of God grow within your soul.

And just as the day arrives when the blessed oyster is ready to share her pearl, so will ye have pearls of wisdom within the heart to share with the world.

Dealing with the Waves of Emotion

Beloved One, to allow the Christ Light to flow within your life is something like the process of sitting in tranquillity at the beach with peace in your heart and observing the ocean waves coming in and bringing with them treasures of shells and all manner of things that come from the sea.

There is a rhythm to this magic, this harmony, this beauty of nature. There is a wise intelligence governing nature in all that she does and all that she encompasses.

Nature is peaceful and brings healing to the soul and to the emotions.

Emotions can come and go like ocean waves.

Sometimes they can roll you over and rob you of your feelings of control. You seem to be able to do nothing other than ride with the pull and flow of the powerful waves.

There are times when it can be joyous to be overcome by the waves of emotion—and there are times when such a loss of control leads to shame, humiliation, and great distress.

When you are centered in the Christ Light, waves of emotion can pass over you and leave you untouched by their force. You cannot be knocked over and pulled off center.

In the strength of the Christ Light, you can always stand your ground against the sudden rush of emotions.

And just as the ocean waves often bring treasures to the shore, so may the waves of emotion bring rewards to those who are centered and not thrown off balance.

But while the waves of the ocean cannot be held back, people do try to hold back their emotions, worrying about what others will think of their reactions.

You should strive to be as natural in dealing with your emotions as is the ocean in its ebb and flow.

Sit in your silent moments and simply listen within.

The ocean of your emotions will speak to you of the treasures of your soul to be washed up and discovered on the shores of your awareness.

Quiet the mind and know that we angels are surrounding you with love.

Some of your emotions may be as a treasure long lost at sea.

Some of your gifts may lie forgotten under deep waters.

Come with us, Beloved One, and we shall assist you in rediscovering the gifts of your soul.

Each Moment Is a Fresh Chance to Start Anew

Beloved One, like the appearance of new spring blossoms, so is each moment an opportunity from the divine to seek new awareness and to partake of the miracle of new birth.

Each moment is a fresh chance to start anew and to appreciate the love and beauty of each other.

It is never too late to start taking small miracles for granted.

When your consciousness is centered in the Light,

you can bless others with your smile, your inner and outer beauty, and the cheerful sparkle in your eyes.

You can be as a new spring bloom that has broken through the cold ice and snow of pain and illusion. Let the beauty of your light flow from within and have the courage to be true to yourself.

The smallest flowers of nature are products of God's paintbrush and profound miracles.

Bless others with the bloom of your own inner beauty.

Be a subtle blessing of light that helps others to see the same reflection of beauty in their own being.

While Rooted on Earth, the Soul Reaches Upward

Beloved One, consider the tall pine tree that reaches up to the sky above. Its roots have run deep into the earth to give support to the strong trunk and allow it to resist wind, rain, cold, and heat.

The mighty tree stands majestic and tall, reaching up to the sunshine above. It freely permits the light to fill its being, for all living things are manifestations of the light force.

There is only one light, but it has many expressions.

The roots of the pine tree are deeply connected to

the Earth Mother, just as you are, Beloved One. Your spiritual roots are a gift from God that shall keep you centered and connected as you come more and more to realize the powerful being of light that you are.

The trunk of the tree, which can be likened unto your body and your being, is held strong and steady by the Divine Light against all the weathering of life on the earth plane.

The many boughs of the tree reach high for the light, just as your soul reaches high for the Creator, ever striving for more light and more knowing.

As the tree has many aspects to its being, so do you.

Its magnificence creates a blessing for all to see. It sets forth an example simply by being.

Not all may truly understand the complexities of its beauty, its magnificence, but one is blessed by looking upon its being.

In like manner, you should not worry whether or not all others shall comprehend the complexities of your being.

All that matters is that others are blessed by the example of your love.

CHAPTER EIGHT

~

Achieve Inner Peace

Softly, gently, comes the heavenly feathered wing beats of the Dove of Peace.

Surely and steadily upon its luminescent path of light comes the Dove of Peace for all hearts to know.

Each beat of its beauteous wings is like a beat from the heart of God for all to feel.

Within its beak the Dove of Peace carries a long-stemmed pink rose, whose very fragrance wafts love and peace into each heart.

The center of the rose represents the Light of God.

Each petal symbolizes the heart of each child of light who walks upon Earth.

Gracefully, the Dove of Peace comes as a bird of white light that brings the message of infinity and light—that each knowing heart is comprised of pure love and pure light.

The dove, the eternal symbol of the peace of God, seeks to fly into each heart, bringing light where before there had been only darkness.

Beloved One, know that the flight of the Dove of Peace is continuous, self-sustained, and everlasting. She comes to sow peace, to plant love, to cultivate trust, faith, compassion, and charity.

Her wings beat sure and steady, seeking to encompass the entire planet in light, as she herself is light.

The dove of the Light of Christ comes to bring a new elegance of being to each heart. It comes to bring an awareness that enlightenment may live within each heart.

An Angelic Meditation of Peace

Beloved One, I bring you a meditation of peace.

Visualize in your imagination a cool, refreshing waterfall, such as might be found in the mountains amongst tall, stately green pine trees.

Know that from this waterfall issues the very energy of serenity, tranquillity, peace, and love.

Know that you may step into the water and feel it wash over you. The water that flows over rocks onto your body has a velvety, smooth feeling to it.

Allow it to wash over your entire being, healing you, centering you, balancing you.

Let this energy fill your being, allow yourself to be encompassed within the Angelic Aura that radiates from this marvelous waterfall.

Let peace fill your soul.

We angelic beings know that in your hectic hustle-and-bustle world, you often become so exhausted that you become out of touch or out of balance with these essential energies of tranquillity and peace. We come to return these soothing energies to you.

Imagine now that you hear angelic music swelling up around the waterfall and that you see a mist of white light swirling around you.

Know that when you walk again through the waterfall, you will receive a wonderful healing and a centering of your being.

Now allow yourself to walk through the misty waterfall of light and feel the cool waters washing over you, cleansing you, soothing you.

Feel the shift in your energies as you walk through this flow of healing light.

Visualize now that behind the waterfall is a cave. Within the cave are many candles glowing in a soft, white light. There are hundreds of candles set upon little ledges in the cave walls.

Take a moment to observe all the beautiful candles softly glowing.

There is a gentle flow of white light that fills the cave throughout its twists and turns.

While the physical eyes might at first perceive the cave as dark, it really is not. It is softly illuminated with love.

Know and understand that this is a special place of meditation that we angels have given you and that you may come here in your mind at any time.

Let all tension fall away from you as you feel God's peace fill you and heal you, balancing you and centering you.

See before you now a smooth path of light that you know you can follow.

Slowly, filled with peace and wonder, you step forward, following many sparkles of white light that seem to beckon you.

You may safely proceed.

Have no fear.

Know that I, Michael, am with you always.

Now see that you have come to a place in the cave that has a circle of light in the center of the path. Know that this is a circle of wholeness that can completely balance your entire being.

Sit within the circle of wholeness and light.

Meditate.

Breathe deeply and let the light of divinity fill you.

Within this centered state of calm, you shall receive clearly.

This is a special place. Allow yourself to be the instrument of God's pure love that you truly are.

When you are ready, simply arise and flow upward through the light that issues to the cave from above.

Let yourself rise up.

Ascend into the vibration of God's peace and love.

Go forward and shine the peace of the Christ Light to others. You shall then see the beauty of their souls in their eyes.

The Wonder of a Trumpeter Swan in Flight

Flowing elegantly through the currents of air, moving on the wing tips of love and light, is the white Trumpeter Swan. Such a being, when airborne, is the pure definition of grace, poise, and flow.

Beloved One, know you that when such a one is in flight, every feather, every nuance and element of its being is involved in the process.

Each aspect of its essence works together as a single creation of God's beauty. From the tip of its beak to the end of its feathered tail, from its webbed toes to its keen eyes, it soars naturally and instinctively.

Beloved One, I now wish you to envision the beauty of this sky being in your mind's eye and to feel the sensation of watching a swan in flight.

For a moment, I ask you to think of nothing else. Allow your mind to be encompassed in the sheer, awesome beauty of this magnificent being.

Now ask yourself if you can live as one who is natural and sure of self.

Ask if you can live as one who naturally and without question accepts self and the God Light within.

Allow your intuitive knowing to flourish as God's voice within your own being. Be centered, not whipped back and forth by the winds of others' words and opinions that may not be your truth.

Stand in God's truth—the gift within your own heart.

As the elegant swan rises in flight from the clear waters of the lake, allow the pure love and the pure light of your soul essence to rise above material concerns.

Be confident of God's Light within you.

Know that you are always guided and never alone.

Let the sweetness of your soul express its grace through the look in your eyes, the glow in your heart, the compassionate touch of your hand on that of another.

Remember well that there is always someone who faces challenges far more difficult than your own.

Observe again the swan. See how it appears to take much delight in the activities of its flight. It would seem to have many moments of peace and calm as it glides surely along the waters of the lake.

Comfortably, without inner struggle, it follows the plan of God within its own instincts.

Allow yourself to be in many ways like unto the wondrous and elegant swan.

Revel sometimes in the wonder and the creativity of the light within you.

Other times, permit your self simply to listen to the voice within, then just know, just be.

Know that all there is around you is part of God's plan.

Yes, Beloved One, strife does exist upon Earth, but such conflicts are not caused by the God Light.

Calm yourself.

Quiet yourself.

Center yourself—and you shall find yourself in a different space from the chaos around you.

You always have a choice of how you choose to react to life's challenges. And remember, you are never alone. The angelic host is always with you.

Share Your Inner Peace with All

Beloved One, never think in terms of return when

you give to another through your heart. Rather, express to your fellow being a thought such as this: "Please accept the love that I give unto you and pass it on to another so that person may pass the love to yet another."

We angels envision a world of the many humans holding hands and sharing love so that it stretches around the planet.

In truth, even now we have many, many angels encircling Earth and holding hands in peace around the globe.

Beloved One, know that peace can be!

Peace is born within the heart. Go forth and live peacefully as an example for others.

Share your peace not only with your fellow humans, but with all that you see, including animals, birds, reptiles, and insects.

Dive Deeply Within when Emotional Waters Are Rough

Beloved One, we angels know that sometimes during the process of life on Earth, the emotional waters get rough and choppy. When this occurs, dive down deep into the waters of your soul and submerge yourself in the love that we feel for you.

Here, within the peace of your heart, you may

leave behind the strife of the surface waters of life. Here you can be calm and at peace from the emotional storms that life on Earth often presents.

When you are at peace within, you are able once again to sense the higher etheric frequencies of light and to anchor yourself in our steadfast, unconditional love.

Let the Christ Light Break Through the Storm Clouds of Illusion

Beloved One, we angels know that at times the busyness of everyday Earth life can seem akin to storm clouds that have gathered in the sky above.

Sometimes when we observe the competitiveness of your business world, we wonder if in some instances there can ever be space for the light to manifest.

In most of the homes that we visit, we see that there is usually love expressed for family and friends. But, sadly, we take notice that the smiles, the love, the light shining through the eyes, are very often left at the doorstep in the morning. We, too, seldom perceive love, smiles, and joy within the confines of the workplace.

Even those who may practice the centering of the Christ Light in their homes very often do not carry this energy with them when they are away from home.

Too often we perceive that the work environment is a place where there is pressure, the jostling of egos, the clash of personalities, and the struggle for control.

It is no wonder that you humans are often so exhausted and so weary.

Although we trust in God's Divine Plan, we sometimes ponder the question of just *when* the day will come when there will be an all-encompassing and unconditional acceptance of one human being for another upon your planet.

To truly center in the Christ Light is to allow the spirit of love and peace for yourself and your fellow human beings to radiate from your heart *wherever* you are.

If you radiate this love in the workplace, other humans cannot help feeling it. The radiation of your love energy will assist them in shifting their own energies.

Let the bells of love joyfully ring forth to cut through illusion and untruth on Earth.

Please allow us angels to show you the purity of the higher realms of light all around you.

Be silent.

Relax and calm your mind through soft music and meditation.

You will always find us present to communicate with you through your heart.

Do not enter the silence with preconceptions.

Do not force peace within.

Do not approach meditation with expectations.

Just let go, and we shall be there for you.

Know that wherever you are, beauteous angels of light are with you each and every moment—ever-ready to inspire, love, and help you to feel the Light of God within.

We are *real*, and we are always *here*.

Enter the silence of meditation, and you shall see the light break through the gray clouds of illusion.

Look up, and allow us to raise your consciousness above the muck of pettiness, selfishness, and competitiveness in the world today.

Walk the path of illusion for the last time. We shall allow the silvery white dove of peace to alight upon your shoulder from the heavens above.

Remember what I have taught you, Beloved One. The peace of the heavens exists also in your heart.

You shall always feel the truth of this in your meditations.

We shall wrap you in our love, and you shall feel this love within.

When the brand-new golden chick finally hatches

from the darkness within the egg and sees the light of the outer world, it is never to be the same again.

Such is the journey of the soul when higher consciousness has been achieved. It can never again return completely to the darkness of illusion.

Celebrate the Gift of God's Love

Beloved Child of God, celebrate yourself. Celebrate the gift of God's love.

Love one another. Love all of creation, for it is sacred in the eyes of God.

Know that within the Christ Light is the central palette of the colors of your heart and soul. Here there exist brushes of many shapes and sizes with which you may paint the scenes of your journey upon Earth.

Allow yourselves to be playful. Envelop yourselves in the simple joys of life.

Allow yourselves to laugh.

Consider one another with thoughtfulness and love.

Banish the common stereotypes, categories, and boxes for your fellow humans that society places upon you.

Be childlike and truly feel the innocence that children convey.

Rise above the limitations of the human state, and let love be the guidance from your heart.

Practice being in the present moment.

Understand that time is an illusion.

Past, present, and future exist in every passing second.

There truly is only an eternal *now*.

Be in the now, and be within the flow of the healing Christ Light.

And Lo, There Was Light Upon the Mountaintops

Beloved One, it was I, Michael, who inspired you to go for a walk in the fields back and above your home. I wished you to perceive an illustration of a great truth.

You know that as you stood at that particular elevation you enjoyed a sweeping view of the entire Rocky Mountain Front Range. From that elevation you could perceive that while the Sun brought its brilliant light to the mountaintops, the plains below were shrouded in heavy clouds of gray. To your perception the contrast was spectacular.

Beloved One, you wonder what the lesson may be. You know that universal, all-encompassing love is the highest vibration that exists. Just as the peaks of the

167

Rocky Mountains reach ever upward toward the illu-mination of the Sun, so does the Light of God shine upon the mountaintops of higher consciousness.

Know this truth: No matter how weather conditions may appear, no matter if you can perceive sunshine or clouds, there is always light above the clouds.

In like manner, the Light of God shines always above the dark clouds of illusion. The Christ Light is always there to banish the fog banks of confusion and error.

Beloved One, reach for the light. It may not always be able to be seen by human eyes, but it is always there.

Feel the light within your heart.

See it within the smile and the eyes of another human being.

Feel it within the love of your pets.

Everywhere there is the light and love of God. Look above the gray clouds of illusion no matter where you are or what you are doing.

Escape Three-Dimensional Reality

Beloved One, allow yourself to relax during your meditational time of light. Permit yourself to feel the wondrous sensation of light filling you and lifting your consciousness ever higher.

We of the Angelic Realms observe how weary and

tired you humans become in your day-to-day lives. We see how you often complain that there is so much to do and that it cannot be accomplished in a twenty-four-hour day.

We angels know that time is an illusion. You see, in our realms, there is no time or space.

Time is a concept that is unique to your planet Earth, and we perceive that it is necessary in order for you to grow and to experience third-dimensional reality.

When you center yourselves during your meditations and prayers, you have become one with an infinite, unlimited, and eternal source of light.

While you are engaged in meditation or prayer, you have escaped three-dimensional reality.

While you meditate or pray, the eternal light flows down through the top of your head, filling every cell down to your toenails and back up to your skull. Finally, the light so permeates your aura that it can contain no more—then the beautiful light flows out of you like a brilliant, sparkling fountain of energy.

This is what we angels behold as we see you center within the Christ Light. The radiance that is you steadily becomes more and more brilliant.

The more that you love, care, share, and help one another, the brighter a beacon of loving light your aura becomes.

A Meditation of Peace, Balance, and Enlightenment

Beloved One, think of yourself standing near a clear mountain lake.

Imagine a clear, blue sky and puffy white clouds on a day full of sunshine.

Imagine the elegance and serenity of tall, green pine trees, gently swaying in the breeze.

See around you a shoreline sprinkled with smooth rocks on a sandy beach.

The lake is so clear that you can see to the bottom.

Feel the peace within you now as you envision this lovely mountain lake where there is no noise, no air or water pollution, no negativity—only the peace for which your soul longs.

The mountain lake that you envision in your mind is a masterpiece created by the God Force.

In your imagination, see yourself sitting upon a large, smooth rock near the shoreline.

Close your eyes and listen.

Simply listen and feel.

Feel the peace, the balance, the alignment, and the attunement flow through you.

Feel the Christ Light, the purity that is always available to you within.

Listen to the birds. Hear the sounds of a chipmunk joyously cavorting near your feet.

Feel peace, Beloved One. Feel peace washing over your entire being with a velvety smoothness.

Know that you are one with this place.

Know that it is one with you as you center within the Light.

At one frequency or another, all things are expressions of some level of light.

Take this beautiful mountain lake with you in your heart and mind wherever you may go.

The clear lake water is like your soul when you calm your emotions in meditation.

When the waters of your emotions are calm, Beloved One, it is easier for those of us of the Angelic Realms to come closer to you and to blend with your level of awareness so that we may relate more to one another.

When the waters of your emotions are restless, unsettled, and choppy, it is more difficult for us to see clearly into your soul.

Be calm and centered, and we can reflect upon your soul more clearly and better assist you in your growth.

Fill your heart with our love and inspiration. Be as peaceful as the clear and serene mountain lake.

The Challenge of Growth

The dance of light and love moves through every living thing. Within each soul is the challenge and adventure of growth.

The challenge begins at birth, and we angels know that it requires great effort to emerge into a new level of light.

For centuries we have observed similar challenges for new generations of humankind. Within the age-old process of being uplifted into a new way of being, a new attitude, a new level of light, we have witnessed much pain as shifts in awareness occur.

Always remember that no one can be you as well as you can.

Yet we know that it takes courage to break away from the classifications, restrictions, and limitations that others would strive to impose upon you. We stand ever near to supply you with that courage and to applaud your efforts to escape the labels and expectations of others.

As you listen to the voice within, heed the comforting admonition that the Light is always there to lead you.

Calm yourself and take the time to feel the Light within.

CHAPTER NINE

Stay Afloat Upon the Waters of Life

Beloved One, consider with me the small leaf that so delicately floats atop the waters of a still mountain lake.

The leaf does not sink. Indeed, it floats serenely atop the water.

It is at peace.

It is quiet and still.

It matters not to the leaf who is or who is not aware of its presence, for God knows.

The angels know.

The I AM THAT I AM knows.

This little leaf floats on crystal-clear waters. See the leaf in your mind, Beloved One.

Imagine a leaf, still and quiet, floating in a mountain lake, drifting along without a thing upon its consciousness other than light.

Yes, all things have the consciousness of light that is God—even a leaf.

The leaf shares life with millions of others of its kind upon the planet—and yet all leaves are one upon the trees of life.

This little leaf that now floats calmly upon the water of a mountain lake is made of the love and beauty of God, just as you are.

Beloved One, allow yourself to be and to feel like this little leaf.

Permit the complexities of life to fall away from you each day in meditation.

Breathe deeply and relax.

Allow yourself to float upon the waters of life and light that exist to support you.

Yes, it may take some courage and faith to let go of all your many concerns. Ask—and all shall be given to you.

Beloved One, take a moment now to envision yourself as this beautiful, safe—yet vulnerable—little leaf that has allowed itself to let go and to float down from the secure tree branch to which it was attached.

The leaf trusted, let go, and floated to the waters below—where it was gently accepted.

Now it continues on its journey.

It asks not why.

It simply is.

In the silence of your meditation, allow yourself to be as the little leaf. In letting go and relaxing, you shall find new awareness. New light shall enter your mind and your being.

Although there is but one light, it expresses itself in many ways.

The light may come to you as visions, as awareness, as intuition, as inspired creativity.

There are a million and more expressions of the Christ Light as you center within it.

There Is No Failure Within the Light of God

Within the Light of God there is no failure.

There is only experience.

There are only lessons.

There is only growth—much of which may only be fully understood and completely known on the soul level.

It is through the process of daily centering within the Light that one begins to remember and to awaken to those goals known on the soul level.

Remember always that you are magnificent. You

are divine and you express your divinity through physical expression.

When you come to those points in your life when you are not certain where to take your next step, look to the heavens for your help. Look within, and the answer shall manifest before you.

As you center in the Light and listen within, you shall see clearly what your next step will be, how to accomplish your goal, and how to move on to accept the next challenge.

Fear not, for we angels care for you. We are always willing to help you to see clearly the unique, special pathway of light that you should follow.

The Light of God within you shall always give you perfect guidance.

Discover the Nest of Light Within Your Heart

Beloved One, recall the time when you discovered the small, brown, well-built bird nest hidden within the tall, green grasses. It was filled with tiny, blue-green eggs of new birth yet to be realized.

Although the nest was unseen by others until your discovery, the mother bird had been protecting the eggs, keeping them warm and safe, preparing for the birth and new being of the chicks.

Beloved One, within your heart is a nest of light, awaiting the birth of new knowledge within your heart.

You are loved.

You are safe.

You are protected.

Always you are nurtured and watched over as new birth appears, as the shells of old beliefs and false self-perceptions crack and fall away. And the love of the angels is ever-present to keep you warm and to guide you.

You see? We watch over you as if we were your surrogate parents.

Listen and follow the inspirations that you receive.

Celebrate your being, your value.

Experience.

Discover.

You are one with the dance of light, love, and life. Know that you are precious to us and that we know your every need.

The Crown Jewel of Consciousness

Within the vast, deep ocean of consciousness that exists within you is the knowledge that you are one with the heart of God.

The Crown Jewel of Consciousness that lies deep

within, awaiting discovery among the waters of being, is the awareness that you are one with the heart of the Source of All-That-Is—and it lies yearning for you to dive deep enough to perceive it within your heart.

As you center within the Light, more treasures of the heart shall be yours as you bring them up into the open air of awareness from the depth of the waters of consciousness. As you discover more jewels of wisdom, you shall experience a shift within your own consciousness.

Yet the Crown Jewel of all is your love of God and the knowledge of your oneness with the Source.

You will not achieve such knowing from the intellect, from your mental faculties. Such wisdom comes from the heart.

As you sit or lie quietly and breathe deeply, meditating upon the love of God, you shall know of the intimate interconnection of all things.

The Clarion Call of Light

Beloved One, the call has sounded forth!

Pay heed to the call of Light sent forth by the ethereal, eternal Angelic Force.

Listen to the clarion call of Light sounded by angelic trumpets of love.

The angels on high wish you to awaken and to know that the light within each heart is that of God's love.

The angels of love want you to know that you and God are a part of one another.

From the Angelic Light in the heavens, the call sounds forth from luminescent trumpets and sparkles like pearlescent notes of music as it travels to Earth and moves all around the planet, singing, "Awaken, awaken to the Christ Light."

The peace and love within your heart shall one day become a reality for everyone!

The planet is surrounded by Angels of Light; and all around the Earth golden trumpets sound from many sacred places where high vibrations exist.

Earth is rising in the vibration of love.

Although it may presently be experiencing labor pains such as those that accompany any new birth process, peace shall be the beautiful result.

A new morning is dawning within each heart that awakens to the love of God within.

Beloved One, understand that there is much more occurring around you on the etheric levels than will ever be seen by those who write your headlines and broadcast your news.

Love is opening new hearts everywhere.

The Tree of Humanity

Envision a tall, majestic pine tree that has stood proud and resisted the rigors of time and weather for many, many years. Its roots are deep within the earth, holding it steady, bringing it nourishment, while it reaches high for the sunshine and blue skies.

Envision humanity as such a beautiful and grand tree.

The center trunk is the God Force, and the many branches of humanity stretch far out from the central source that is present upon the earth plane.

Upon each branch are many thousands of pine needles, representing millions of people.

Each element of the tree is necessary to create the totality of itself.

In like manner, all humans are as one within the great I AM presence, the oneness that is God. Each person is a child of God and is necessary to create the totality of Earth.

Remember always that all are one, and let the God Light within you radiate through your eyes and through your smile for your fellow human beings.

Meditate Upon the One and All Things Shall Be Given to You

Beloved One, meditate upon the Oneness.

Within the oneness exists the ultimate journey of light.

And remember always that it is only on the journey that your growth commences, not when the destination has been reached.

Meditate upon the One, and all shall be given to you through the gifts of your soul.

Gifts of the soul are to share, for they are the essence of spiritual love.

Does not the harp become more fine-tuned with use and practice?

Does not the heart become more of a beacon light when it is shared with your fellow beings?

Love heals all, sustains all, refreshes all.

Love gives courage and strength to the spirit to soar above the hills and the valleys and to come home to full union with God.

When you begin to meditate upon the oneness that you share with All-That-Is, you center within the Light of the One. You are then able to share your light and to live by the example of love.

Envisioning a Heart-Shaped Earth

Envision Earth as one enormous heart with oceans, land, people, animals, birds, plant life, light, love, and indescribable beauty. National boundaries are illusions, existing only in the minds of some.

Now envision this heart-shaped planet with a heart

of her own—a heart that radiates love and peace to all who live upon her surface with love and peace.

The Earth is your planetary mother. Would you not treat your mother with love and respectful consideration?

Beloved One, help others come into this awareness. Love your planet and treat it with the profound respect that you should show toward your dear mother.

The Human Symphony

Beloved One, one might say that God is the director of the orchestra that is humankind. Each precious human being is an instrument of light, and each being is learning that it is only through the humble instrumentality of service that fine-tuning can occur.

Oh, what a blessing to hear a symphony orchestra in harmony, with each musician in sync with one another, playing together as one.

There are, of course, many sections, many parts, many elements within a symphony.

Each instrument has its own mission to perform to make the music perfect.

When all the harps, violins, trumpets, flutes, drums, and so forth, are brought together under the sure hand of the director, exquisite beauty results and the ears, minds, and hearts of the listeners are truly blessed.

So it is when all people can relate in harmony and bring their many experiences together as one, working in love and compassion, can blessings result for the highest good of all concerned.

When all humanity realizes through the heart that all are one, then can the many different musical scores of life become the one masterpiece directed by the one Master Director, with whom all are one.

Seek Not the Guru on the Mountaintop

Beloved One, know that the light of God flows through your wondrous, luminescent, translucent body of light.

Know that the beauty of your soul is the reflection of the God Light within you.

The grandeur of the natural spiritual magnificence that you are *now* is enlightenment in and of itself.

Rather than seeking the all-knowing Guru on the mountaintop, seek within—and you shall be given the truth that you desire.

Allow God to guide each momentous moment. Completely let go and let God lead you to clarification in meditation and in prayer and in joy in your lifestream.

Each experience in your life brings forth a lesson of the soul that instructs you, tests you, challenges you.

All are teachers, and all are students.

Maintain a high level of your thoughts, words, and actions.

Share love with your fellow beings.

Share an act of kindness that might touch someone's heart.

Share the warmth of your smile that can melt the ice of a hardened heart.

Not everyone may understand or appreciate the level of your love. That is all right. Remember well that it is the example you set that truly matters.

An angel's love is all-encompassing, unconditional, and given to help a soul without the expectation of return.

In like manner must you give love automatically—simply for the sake of love that is love.

Listen within, and you shall know how God chooses to have you become an instrument of service.

Center within every day through meditation and prayer.

Be in tune with the higher light.

Compare yourself to no other human and judge not your value according to others—for better or worse, richer or poorer, higher or lower.

Know that in the eyes of the angels, you are special and unique.

Know also that there is no separation in the God Force of Love between you and every other living thing.

CHAPTER TEN

We Are All Beings of Light

Within your true essence, you are light.
You are love.
You are one with all beings of light.

You Hold Within You the Perfect Thought of God

To center within the Christ Light is to allow the eternal waterfall of illumination to flow down from the heavens and into your very being. This marvelous source of light ever awaits your invitation.

To center within the Christ Light is to permit yourself to be loved, treasured, and appreciated as the child of God that you are.

To center within the Christ Light is to receive angelic light and love unconditionally without the ill-defined categories and thought forms of human society.

You are a child of God who holds within you the perfect thought of God, the pure light that is yet un-qualified within human activity.

The energies on which you place your attention are qualified within your own words, actions, and thoughts.

Think on this statement for a moment, for it is a powerful truth.

We angels are always there to assist you to keep your words and deeds sincere and balanced.

The I AM Affirmations

Beloved One, I, Michael, share with you these I AM affirmations of great power and light.

I AM that I AM in All that I AM within all cre-ation, within all that is God Force, all that is one.

I AM the presence of light within each heart.

I AM the stability from which all of life draws its creative breath.

I AM the golden sunshine from each soul that cen-ters within the Christ Light.

I AM the pure white light of the Christ that sur-rounds and balances everyone.

I AM the purity of the awakening rose within everyone.

I AM love, the most powerful force of good that exists.

I AM the breeze in the trees, the clouds in the skies, the sunshine and the rain.

I AM the song of the bird, the symphony of the frogs upon the lily pads, the serenade of the wolf cry to the Moon.

I AM the moonlight at the water's edge, the snowflakes falling silently upon the land, the new blossoms of spring.

I AM all of Nature, the great teacher of healing and love.

I AM always everywhere. Listen within your heart and know that you are a part of God and that God is a part of you.

I AM always with you, for you are a precious child of the Universe, learning and growing upon Earth.

I AM the one who sends my angels to watch over you.

Nature provides the silence from which your heart speaks the truth that is individually yours.

All is one within you. All is interconnected to the light in your heart.

Give love, and it shall multiply unto you.

Next to the Light, All Else Is Illusion

Beloved One, when you are in meditation, envision yourself as a pine cone that floats upon the surface of a still, calm pond of the clearest water that you can imagine.

See yourself as that pine cone floating quietly on the waters. The day is filled with sunshine that reflects off the water in many sparkles of light.

Thus is how it feels when one is truly centered within the light. It is as if one is floating in balance and calmness and supported by the waters of tranquil emotion.

What a scene of beauty and clarity!

When you are so centered, we angels are able to see right to the depths of you, just as you imagining yourself to be the pine cone could see clearly down through the depths of the clear water.

This beauty, this light, is the real you.

All else in the outer world is illusion when it is next to the Light.

When you are centered within the Light, there is not a ruffle upon the waters of your emotions.

The Unlimited Horizons of God's Love

Beloved One, sometimes when you were driving your automobile across great distances, you felt as though the road before you seemed to go on and on.

As you drove on, you oftentimes could not see the horizon—and when you finally got to where you thought the horizon was, the road now stretched even farther into what appeared to be an infinite, unlimited horizon.

This is the way of God's eternal love that lives within your heart. It stretches forth into infinity, for you, yourself, are an eternal being of light.

The road of life that you travel on Earth offers many different kinds of scenery and many different experiences to encounter.

But the Light of God is constant. And with each new horizon that you experience, the Christ Light awaits you, bringing fresh blessings for your soul's nourishment.

All roads lead to God.

All beliefs, all truths of light lead to God.

There is no up or down, no better or worse.

The Christ Light is in all that you see. All are one with All-That-Is.

All are a part of God.

Do Not Hold Another in Judgment

Beloved One, you are a magnificent, powerful, spiritual being of light and of love. Therefore, never judge another. The specific reasons for the lifepath of another human being is known only in the higher realms.

When humans hold others of their kind in judgment, they may very well attract the energy that they have judged into their own experience in order to achieve balance.

They may have drawn unto themselves the necessity to "walk a mile in the shoes" of the one that they have judged.

They may have set in motion a physical law that requires them to know exactly how the other person felt in that situation.

Forgive with love and bless others, knowing that God will administer all the lessons that one must learn along the path.

And understand that you can never pull others along their path—or tug them onto your own path, for each life walk is different.

In the Higher Realms, for reasons unknown to you humans, there is no right or wrong—only experience.

Regardless of how you may have perceived someone as wronging you, know that the God Force has observed the action and will bring about the required balance.

It is not up to you to take steps of correction.

God knows.

The angels know.

Your soul knows.

All-That-Is shall administer the necessary lessons for that one's soul growth.

A Wondrous Flower that is Blooming

Beloved One, sometimes I think of you as a wondrous flower that, while rooted in the earth, blooms and grows ever higher toward the light.

Your soft fragrance wafts along the breeze to many others of your kind, inspiring them to reach toward the light.

The golden center of the flower that is you is like the Golden God Light within your heart. The delicate petals that unfold for only a moment in God's knowing are like the many aspects of yourself that flow out from your heart.

The wondrous flower lifts its face upward toward the sunshine—the Light of God that comes to warm all.

Meditate upon the beauty within your heart.

How to Receive More Christ Light

Beloved One, here are some ways to help you receive more Christ Light in your heart:

Express humbleness of heart.

Express gratitude of the heart and of your ensoulment, which is the Higher God Essence of Yourself.

Know that all comes first from God in energy form that is pure. How you express this light energy and qualify it depends upon your own free will.

As above so below. That which you express on Earth shall always return to the Creator in the higher realms.

Remember that all that is comes *first* from the pure light of the Higher Spiritual Realms, *then* through humanity, not *vice versa*.

Allow yourself to be an instrument of God's light to bless and to enlighten others upon the planet.

Many are called into service, but few are chosen.

To be chosen, simply choose yourself.

Everything light-filled and good is in service to the One. Anything done in the spirit of love, regardless of how lowly or menial, is of service to God. Simply do the best that you can do at whatever you are doing in the present moment.

Keep a special place in your heart in which to hear your inner God Light speaking with you.

There are a million truths and a million ways home to God. Choose the truth and the way that is right for you.

Test the words of others within your heart.

If the words of others resonate within you, they are also right for you.

If they do not seem to resonate within your essential self, discard them and listen and search until you do find what is right for you.

All answers are to be found within, in the inner realms.

No one person expressing through human physicality shall have all the answers.

There exist many beliefs, many religions, many spiritual paths. Each have some truth that leads home to God.

Remember that the only place where *all* answers are found is the God Light within you.

Meditate and listen.

Let go, and the answer will appear.

The answer may not always be what you wish to hear, but it will be an expression of God's direction and path for you to follow.

Judge not another's path, for how can one entity who is expressing the physicality of the earth plane know the lessons and growth patterns intended for another human's ensoulment? Only God knows the many soul-chosen paths of spiritual evolution.

Allow the I AM that I AM to restore divine order to all situations and to lead you aright.

Do the best you can with your lessons at hand. Release the rest to God.

Most importantly, trust the beauty and divinity that you are.

Receive These Gifts of Love and Light

These things are given unto you:

Love

Faith

Patience

Charity

Forgiveness

Peace

Trust

Compassion

Empathy

Beloved One, being of service upon the planet in small, as well as, great ways is valid and valuable. All thoughts, words, and deeds are known by the heavens above.

It is important that you love, value, and respect self and others.

Listen to your soul.

Listen to others.

Love one another.

It matters not who you are or what you are

195

doing—*love one another, truly, sincerely, with your heart.*

Take no person or event for granted.

Express your love for others and yourself today. Do not wait for opportunities to go by or have regrets for what might have been.

And love not with the ego or with the mind—but with your heart.

We angels shall sometimes visit you in disguise, and you will not always know how much you have blessed another with the simplest acts or words of love.

Be a Prism for the Light of God

All of the human entities on Earth have the capability of multiplying their inner light many times over the light-refracting properties of a prism.

Place a crystal or a prism in a window filled with sunshine, and you shall see rainbows of color illuminating the room.

In like manner, when your heart is clear and open, the spiritual light and power of God can shine through and fill your world with rainbows.

Each human being may be a wondrous instrument for the gifts of Light that God can bestow.

Love the God within before you embark upon any thought, word, and deed.

Pray for right action, right words, and right thoughts.

Pray for the I AM that I AM to guide you in all things at all times.

As light flows through a crystal or a prism, all human beings can permit the love of God to flow through them and bring the rainbow of inspiration to all. All humans can become one with the intensity of the light frequency of the higher realms.

Beloved One, you have multifaceted abilities like that of a wondrous diamond or crystal. Open up to the marvel of your own soul.

As a prism is an instrument of light that bringeth beauty, let your heart open to be a prism that bringeth forth joy.

Be a prism for God. Let the angels inspire you with their example of luminescent joy, their dance of love.

Radiate your love from within, as a crystal or a prism does when exposed to light from a sunny window.

Beloved One, be in the sunny window of God's love and let the intense frequencies of loving light create colorful rainbows of love as it flows through the prism of your heart.

The One Light of God Has Many Expressions

The one light of God flows and dances through all humanity. It moves through all spheres, all dimensions, all solar systems, all galaxies, and beyond what is known to physical existence.

All that exists is the expression of light in one vibrational frequency or another.

The one light of God has many expressions within all planes of consciousness.

The Christ Light is available for all who will reach for it and open their hearts to love.

Those of us who come from higher realms and who are often referred to as "Beings of Light" know that there is only one light, God's Light. We also are aware that this light moves in ever-increasing frequencies of consciousness, love, and service to humankind.

The Christ Light is perceived individually within the many in an infinite number of ways.

Universally, men and women are led to know that there is a reason and a purpose for them to be upon the earth plane.

In general, they wish to be of greater service to God and to humanity in large and small ways.

Some may wish to teach others and share the insights that they have learned in classes and workshops.

Others may have increased clarity and vision, but wish to share what they know only through the course of daily, informal conversations in the home or in the workplace.

Still others may be led to write books about spiritual truths, angels, the God Force, and other inspirational topics.

And there will be those who will first heal themselves, then seek to assist in the healing of others.

It is truly a time for sharing.

The Light of God and the holy angels will inspire enlightened humankind to find the path of service that best suits the individual.

Service to God comes in many, many forms. It matters not what you do, as long as it is a service to others in the spirit of love and helpfulness.

Do your best at each thing you do—whether it is washing dishes in a restaurant or lecturing to large audiences of spiritual seekers.

Bring a nature of cheerfulness to whatever you do.

It is illusion to think of yourself as separate from others.

Bless your fellow men and women.

Bless the Children of the Light for being the light bearers and teachers that they are.

Send love to all from your heart.

When you help another being in loving service, you grow.

And because you have allowed those of us of the Angelic Realms to be of service in guiding you, we grow as well.

The Rainbow Hues of Hue-manity

Beloved One, I am going to speak to you of *Hue-*mankind.

Each human being is a shading of the color of God.

Each human entity is an aspect of the vibrational frequency of the rainbow of color and light that is God.

All-That-Is is comprised of every color on Earth and of every hue that lies beyond physical sight.

There are shadings of light in the Heavenly Realms that no human eye has ever seen.

Beloved One, know you that there are no divisions within the Higher Realms that are based upon this thought or that belief or on this color or that appearance. Such separations constitute an illusion that is perpetrated on the earth plane, but is not known in the Higher Realms of light frequency.

As I have told you, while all exists of light, there

is only one light that expresses itself through many spheres, dimensions, and planes of thought.

There is only one light, one love, one God, manifesting to you in many millions of ways.

Yes, it is true that the inner voice is individual in each person—yet each is one within the Love of God.

As you live upon the earth plane, fear not your fellow humans.

All people of all hues should be prepared to learn from one another.

All humans of all cultures and societies should allow themselves to be enriched with the experience of knowing one another.

HUE-MANITY.

Honor the HUE of one another.

Seek the truth and the light of the heart within each human being, not the color of the skin, hair, or eyes.

Know that no hue is superior or less than any other.

The common thread, Dear Child of Light, is the hue of God's love that threads through every single human being and sews His tapestry of love.

Honor one another.

Think not that another must walk your path, for

none hath the particular and specific lessons to learn that you must achieve while on the earth plane.

It has been said that you should grow where you are planted, and God alone shall know the time of the blooming of the flower of your heart.

CHAPTER ELEVEN

The God Force Sustains Us All

Beloved One, always be true to your own self. Be authentic unto your own self. Be natural unto your own self.

Have the courage to love yourself just as you are.

While great beauty exists in the world of nature, the more profound subtleties of such beauty speaks only to the awesome splendor that is reflected within your heart and your soul. Any beauty that you behold in the outer world is but a reflection of that wonderfulness that exists within the quiet waters of your soul.

In order to see something reflected outside of your self in the outer world, it must first exist within the inner levels of your heart and your soul.

To experience love, love first your own self.

To experience respect, respect your own self.

Take a walk through nature and silently observe the subtle, as well as the larger, things. Notice the texture of the ground, the tiny plants, the hidden flowers, the crawling insects, the differences between the kinds of trees.

At the same time, take note of the many subleties within yourself—within your heart, soul, and emotions.

Beloved One, urge all your brother and sister humans to find a wooded area, a riverbank, a lake shore, a beach, or a park somewhere near their homes. Bid them to listen, see, smell, and feel deep within as they talk daily in silence through this gift of God and Nature.

Beloved One, whenever you walk in Nature, bring its pure energies and its quiet into your being. Then listen to the quiet within yourself.

As you learn better how to open yourself to the oneness of Nature, you will be able to see even more clearly that you are a spiritual being that is adjusting to being human.

Have Faith and Trust in the Now

Be in the moment.

Live in the present moment.

Love in the Now.

From one moment to the next, the now is all that there is.

Only the God Force has loving control of all things, so have trust and faith in the now—for that is all that is.

Know that within the present moment, within each moment, there is a God who loves each aspect of the whole that is you.

Truly, your being is blessed with many wondrous aspects that are simultaneously active within the physical and spiritual realms.

You are more than you seem to be.

Within the all-encompassing love and grace of the One God, there is growth, forgiveness, light, and joy.

There is courage and strength.

There is active guidance through each moment.

The power of God that has created all things has placed you in cocreation with the loving All-ness at all times.

It is part of the ascension process of each soul to integrate and to balance the physical and spiritual aspects of creation as you walk your path through life.

Beloved One, know that as you expand in individual and collective consciousness throughout the sweet and beautiful Earth, you blossom into a jewel, just as she is. You raise your consciousness into the vaster aspects of yourself—the divinity of God that flows through the heart of each soul.

Each person whose consciousness is lifted through the love of God and the wondrous angelic ones makes the planet a little bit more of the paradise that it once was and shall once again be.

The angelic ones know of this truth, and they strive to bring humans closer to the love within their hearts and guide them back upon the path to the knowing of an intense, yet gentle and deep, love for all.

Love in the present moment.

Savor the wonder and the beauty of each bite of the fruits of light and life.

Let go and let God—and be in the now.

Be One with the Golden Light of the God Force

Beloved One, in your meditations allow the Golden Light of the God Force to flow into your physical embodiment from the top of your head. Visualize the light filling each cell of your being—physically and etherically.

Picture each of the billions of cells within your physical being wearing happy, smiling faces as they move about, their essence filled with the Golden

Light of the God Force. They are individual, yet as one, within the God Force.

See Golden Light flowing from your heart center and filling each of your physical cells with the soothing, calming, comforting balm of golden radiance.

Breathe deeply.

Allow the golden glow to linger within your being from head to toe and everywhere in between.

Allow the light to fill you to the point where you can visualize yourself as flowing like a fountain.

Imagine that you simply cannot hold any more of the light.

See it flowing back out of your physical body through the top of your head.

Picture yourself as if you were a wondrous fountain filling your aura with glorious light.

See yourself so filled to overflowing with the Golden Light that no negative thoughts or energies can be contained within your physical vehicle.

Negative thoughts and emotions may flow by you, around you, even stop momentarily *on* you, but they move on and cannot be held within you.

No negativity can penetrate the Golden Light of the God Force that circulates in and out of you.

Passively observe these energies of negativity and let them flow on away from you.

Beloved One, humans always have a conscious choice whether or not to go to the Light.

Your responsibility is to your own pathway and to raise your own consciousness into the Light.

Allow the Christ Light to Be Your Active Partner

Know full well that within the forest of humanity there are places of dark shadows as well as areas where sunshine comes through the overhanging branches. There are places of rest and there are obstacles—just as a real forest of trees might contain.

When you are centered within the Christ Light and have surrendered completely to its energy, you will be given all.

When you stop trying so hard to conquer life on your own and allow the Christ Light to be an active participant in your struggle, you will be shown so much more of the Universe than you ever dreamed possible.

Ask and you shall receive.

When you permit the Christ Light to be an active partner in your life experience, you shall be given a much larger overview, perspective, and awareness. You will be shown how all things in time and space can be simultaneously possible.

Receive the Pure Energies of the God Force

The energies of the God Force always come to you in absolute purity.

It is up to you as to how you will choose to qualify them with your thoughts, words, and deeds in your interactions with your fellow travelers upon Earth.

Beloved One, lift your eyes to the heavens from which all love cometh.

The heavens await the resonance of your blessings.

Find the Heaven Within Your Heart

Beloved One, lift up your consciousness to find the heaven within your heart.

The light is always on in the heaven within your heart. The light within is like an inextinguishable candle whose golden flame burns ever steadily, consistently, and reliably. It is like a lighthouse on a rocky shore that strongly shines its guiding light over the waters of emotion and of life.

The light in the heaven within your heart is waiting for you to center yourself within the beams of the Christ Light that is projected for you.

The light that is all encompasses all, seen and unseen. It holds within its loving embrace all the mysteries of life.

Beloved One, you well know that all that exists is light on one level or another. Go deep within to enter the heaven within your heart, and you shall discover even more wonders than you have perceived thus far.

The God Force is always waiting to take you higher in consciousness.

The Angelic Kingdom awaits your invitation to assist in the process of your spiritual growth.

The God Force Will Never Fail You

The Christ Light is always ready to encompass each heart within its embrace. The force field of its love contains all wisdom, love, and truth.

Go within your heart and allow the Christ Light to guide you.

Know that the God Force will never fail you.

Listen to the soft, gentle voice within you.

Behold the light of truth.

Beloved One, you know that your own path is individual and is precious to God. You know also that you must respect the pathway and light of all other souls.

One heart healing another will in time make your planet a paradise complete.

I, Michael, and the heavenly hosts of angels stand

always ready to guide you to the truth within your own heart. All you need to do is to ask with a sincere heart—and we shall hear you.

You might ask our help in surrendering to the God Light within you.

You might affirm thusly, "Dear God, I surrender to you. I own not myself—but you do. I surrender. Allow me to be an instrument of thy love. I let go into the trust that, with angelic help, the Christ Light will guide, prosper, bless, and protect me."

The Music of the Christ Light

The music of the Christ Light is to be found in an unlimited multitude of ways.

The simplest way to flow with this heavenly music is to listen within your heart and to recognize that it soars within every person, animal, bird, or thing on the planet.

Every work of creation on Earth carries within it the spark of the Creator.

Let the flow of the Light gently carry you along your pathway of life. Let go and let God help you to distinguish the music, the magic, and the beauty of all of life.

When you completely surrender to the Light of God within your heart, the angels shall care for you in ways that you cannot yet imagine—and in ways far better than you could guess.

The Universe is as safe as the consciousness of your thoughts and the various intentions that you choose to project.

The Christ Light Is Inherent in All Things

Beloved One, know you that the Christ Light is inherent in all things.

All things bright and beautiful upon Earth are an outer expression of the Light of God within each soul.

When you behold something beautiful in another work of God's creation, it is because the Light *must* be within your own being *before* you can recognize it within something or someone else.

We, of the Angelic Realms, wish for each human to know just how lovely and wonderful the God Light within each of you truly is.

As humans, your feet are planted on Earth. But as you awaken to the beauty within you and you look up into the God Light, your awareness and the Christ Consciousness within you is enhanced—and your growth is enriched.

A Guided Meditation from Michael

Beloved One, it is a good thing if within your meditation you visualize your breath moving in and out of your lungs in a deep, circular motion.

Breathe in slowly through the nose. Hold it for a moment.

Then allow the breath to move slowly out of your mouth.

When you breathe in this manner, your physical embodiment shall be more easily filled with life-giving oxygen and the energy of the life force itself.

Allow yourself—slowly, gently, lovingly—to breathe in this way for a moment or a few minutes—until you are relaxed and your mind is quiet.

To breathe in this manner will assist you in the process of centering within.

Breathing in this fashion will always calm the mind and slow you down so that you may properly relax.

Breathing in this fashion—in through the nose and out through the mouth—is recommended also to avoid shallow breathing. In your fast-paced world of Earth, you need always to receive proper amounts of oxygen in order to lessen stress. Consider taking breathing, rather than coffee, breaks. We want you always to be more calm and more centered within the light of your soul.

Here is a short, guided meditation that will refresh you and center you.

Close your eyes, and in your mind, allow the following images to form.

You are sitting on a golden beach of sand.

See yourself sitting in warm, golden sunshine.

Above you is the clear, blue sky. Before you is the ocean with its eternal ebb and flow.

Hear the sound of the waves moving in and out. Hear the cries of the seagulls overhead.

Notice the tiny intricacies of nature all around you. See the little crabs scurrying across the sand. See the shells washed up on the beach.

You see now that there is an etheric ocean of light as well as the physical ocean of water.

The waves of the ocean of light are clear and crystalline. And, as you rise to your feet, you can see that, unlike the physical ocean, you can see directly to the bottom of the etheric ocean.

As far as your eyes can see, you can look straight to the bottom of the ocean of light.

As you gaze into the etheric waters, you know that you have experienced a healing from the beauty that you have perceived. You see truly that you are one with All-That-Is.

As you stand observing the beauty of the etheric

ocean, waters of light begin to move toward shore and to wash over your entire being.

You remain standing, not moving from your physical stance.

Each wave of pearlescent, translucent, golden-white light from the etheric ocean washes over you. Wave after wave moves in from the ocean to move over you.

With each progressive wave of light, you know that you are cleansed and filled with the Christ Light.

After it has moved over you, each wave then flows back into the ocean of light for cleansing and further transmutation.

The waves from the ocean of light have the ability to transmute all that is not of the light into higher, spiritual energy.

Go back to the spot on the beach where you were sitting.

Know that the light of these waters and the light within you are truly one—and one with all that is upon the planet.

Remain in this place for as long as you need.

If you wish, raise your hands to the heavens to be further cleansed and filled with light.

When you are ready, open your eyes and feel joy in your heart and a smile on your lips.

Of Hummingbirds and Light

Today, Beloved One, I would like to speak of hummingbirds and light.

There are no birds on Earth quite like the hummingbird. This tiny bundle of feathers projects power and energy. It has unique abilities to navigate in any direction at any moment, yet it expends so much energy that it must constantly nourish its physical embodiment so it can continue with its flight.

You have beheld how rapidly the wings of the hummingbird move. So fast that human eyes cannot follow the speed of the wing beats. The movement of the wings appear to you as a blur of motion. Its wings are moving at a faster frequency of light than your eyes are able to follow.

Envision, please, Beloved One, the hummingbird as if it were a luminescent bird of light. Envision the tiny, powerful bird of light radiating the sparkles of the true life, which is the reality of the light within the heart.

All creation is nurtured by the love of the Divine. Just as the frequencies of light in the higher dimensions and realms of light are vibrating faster than the physical human eye can usually see, yet the Christ Light is present in all things.

Truly, I often perceive these tiny bundles of bird-joy as if they were angelic representatives for the love and happiness that they bring to others who observe their incredible flight patterns.

Beloved One, they are the only birds on Earth who are able to hover in center position and—should they choose to do so—move up and down, back and forth, as if they were making the sign of the cross.

Every day, every single hummingbird makes the sign of a cross of love and light thousands of times.

Envision the hummingbird in some of your meditative moments. See them centering the light as they do.

God's light is as unlimited to them as it is to you.

Nothing Is Untouched by the Christ Light

Beloved One, as I have told you previously, the Christ Light has begun to flow upon your planet with ever-increasing intensities of love and truth.

The Christ Light is touching every human heart, every animal, every bird, every insect, every plant, every piece of land, every body of water. Nothing is untouched.

The light of All-That-Is is touching every molecule, every aspect of creation on Earth.

The Light of God has a million and more expressions and each one is inexplicably interconnected within the heart of the other.

The focus of God's Light is Love.

Everywhere we angels look, we see an expression of God's love.

You humans may not always be able to see it on the surface of things, for you may largely perceive the pain that is in your world.

We angels, however, see love everywhere. If you could but see with our eyes, you would perceive a magical garden of love existing within each human heart.

Meditate Upon the Image of Your Soul Beauty

Beloved One, know that we angels come to heal, to sustain, to love.

We come to comfort and to bring solace to the soul of each one who is ready to receive the love and the light of the Christ Light. We come to fine-tune the harp strings of light that you are.

In your meditations, Beloved One, look within the clear, crystalline pool of your soul and let the waters be still.

Look deeply within those waters to behold the elegance, the grace, and the beauty that is the soul being within you.

Gaze deeply into those waters and take note of the exquisitive loveliness that you see.

Look closely.

Describe carefully the wondrous reflection from the pool.

What color is the hair, the eyes?

Of what rainbow hue is the robe upon your soul being?

Behold the marvelous shimmer of your soul's sparkle.

Know, Beloved One, that your soul being contains enlightenment and love, wisdom, and knowledge.

The Light of God sustains your every breath.

The Light of God shines eternally into the timeless, infinite, ceaseless perfection that is your inner soul being.

The Light of God knows all destinations simultaneously at once.

Beloved One, meditate upon the image of your soul beauty. Remember, before you took physical embodiment, you knew unlimited freedom in the heavens.

But you knew then—what you have now remembered—that there is no separation from the heavenly home.

There is no separation from the God Force—of which you shall always be a part.

Listen within and let your heart soar.

Let your heart be filled with the love that is you—and which we angels have for you!

Continue Always in the Natural Flow of Your Being

Beloved One, never forget that when the flow of your lifepath happens to encounter obstacles in the road, know that when you call upon the angels and the God Light for help, ways of a higher vibration will always manifest to assist you to continue the natural flow of your being.

Life will always continue to express within God's plan.

Always have faith, for life is filled with miracles if only human eyes are open enough to perceive them.

Heal thyself, and then heal the hearts and souls of others who are willing to heal.

Share your love with all through kindness, a word of compassion, or a gentle touch.

In the Beginning, the Light Flowed Forth

In the beginning, the Light flowed forth and became one with all it created.

The Light—the expression of God's great love for all that is.

The Light—which alone exists on many different levels of dimensional reality.

Beloved One, Light is the intensity of frequency, of consciousness, of love. There is only one light—and light is all that there is.

All existence embodies light on some level, from a very slow vibration to a one so fast that it cannot be perceived with human eyes. That is why some humans can see angels, and others do not.

Beloved One, more exists just beyond the range of human sight than most of you would ever suspect.

You are pure love and pure light—and there is a vast electromagnetic light spectrum-continuum that exists between you and those of us who have come to love you.

The Light that flowed forth in the beginning invites each heart to dance in the fullness of love.

The Light, which knoweth its own, dances in the heavens, and invites all hearts to lift themselves to higher realms so that they might see, know, and be one with the light of all.

My Beloved One, envision a beam from the deepest reaches of space, dancing, flowing forth, and enveloping your beautiful planet in a light that causes all eyes and hearts to look upward and inward.

Envision a beam of light that encompasses all colors of the rainbow—including hues that humanity have not yet seen—and envelops the entire planet within its illumination of love.

This is the many-and-the-one light that floweth forth to call each soul home to God.

Earth is being healed through the light from above.

Know that fear cannot exist within the light from on high—only truth and love.

CHAPTER TWELVE

Find Heaven Within
Your Heart

One morning in January 1995 while I was doing a walking meditation near our home in the Colorado mountains, my dogs Brandy and Laddie and I noticed that we had company.

A huge pink-orange sphere of light hovered in front of us as we walked along—and various colored spheres of light flashed on both sides of us. These spheres of light I could see with my open eyes. I also saw the clear, white bodies of some Light Beings moving about, as well as a rose-colored sphere of light hovering in the trees. The dogs are used to the angels, so they just walked along quietly beside me.

Daephrenocles once told me that I would always have plenty of company when I went out walking.

He said that there would always be Light Beings hovering near me.

For me, heaven is within my heart. I have only to go to the silence within and I am meditating with the angels.

As I go for quiet walks in the natural beauty of my environment, I often think of the words of Daephrenocles, who has admonished me to remain humble in the purity and light of the One.

"Qualify the purity of the One through your thoughts, emotions, and actions," he told me.

Then, continuing with his lesson, he said the following:

Among the angels there is a saying that goes like this: "To know, to dare, to do, and to be silent." Meditate upon those words. Most of all, focus upon the Oneness.

All are one in God's family. All are sisters and brothers of light, for does not all energy return to its creator, its originator, the one who has expressed it?

Let the purity of God's light shine through you and through the wondrous works of light that you do and share.

Go into the Oneness within you. That is your true home, that is where the inner realms of light sparkle and shine awaiting your acceptance, acknowledgment, and awareness.

The greatest truths, the greatest love, the greatest spiritual power are all within—combined with integrity, humbleness, and gratitude.

I feel that I have truly become one with my spiritual expression, my philosophy of love toward all things, and my belief that the unseen world of angelic beings is all around us every minute of every day.

Each day, I strive to live and breathe a mystical union with the angels. My heart is in heaven, and heaven is within my heart.

The Angels' Gifts
By Lori Jean Flory

Softly do we come upon the heartstrings of your divinity, the music of your soul.

We come gently in service and humble gratitude; you honor us with your presence.

Joyously do we come, hovering ever-near upon luminescent, loving wings of purest light.

Softly do we hover around you in robes of light flowing.

We come to fill your hearts with love; and we bear gifts of love.

We are you. You are we. We are magnificent in expression.

Forever do we watch over you, for never are you alone. We are one.

Through the heart we shall help you heal.

Always we will lead you to joy and higher expression.

You are divinity, enlightenment, and perfection of soul. Simply be. Let go—and simply be.

Through surrender to the light within your heart shall come the ecstasy of the Soul.

This is our joyous gift to you, Beloved Doves of our hearts: The One Heart.

Listen within. Remove the lamp shade from the light within and allow your radiance to sparkle and flow.

Without a movement, without a word, see the gift that you are.

The light of the Soul shines through the eyes, through the heart, where no words exist.

We surrounded you in the calm and serene stillness of the crystal blue lake of your Soul. Here the waters of emotion are calm and reflect clearly the true you—and our love.

Through the Angelic Light of your own Soul, of our own God Light, floweth the ecstasy.

An angel's love is the reflection of your heart.

You are the joy-filled symphony, the pure music of the spheres.

Within the heart flow beauteous robes of light and joyous, sparkling wings of love.

Like the musical notes of a symphony, you are each essential to create the ONE.

You are the reasons for our existence. You are angels, too! We simply mirror you.

We come in waves of bright cherubic exuberance to lift you up into your higher light.

An Angel's love creates the perfect space to see your true self within the heart.

We bring you cherubic kisses and gentle angelic caresses of your ears and face.

We come to shower you with blessings divine, like hundreds of soft, dewy rose petals.

Like a pink rose of love, you are blooming, growing upward into heavenly light.

We ask you to remember this: You are divine first—and then wondrously human.

You are the Angels' Gift—for the Angel is you!

No "Tools" Other than My Own Instrument

Interestingly, in all the years that I have undergone angelic attunement and been growing in spirit, the Light Beings have never allowed me to use such "tools" as Tarot cards, Ouija boards, and so forth.

Once in a while, just for myself and no one else, I may pull a rune stone from my bag and look it up in the book, but that's about it. I have never been allowed to touch a Ouija board. There is a big block of energy that flies up between me and the board.

I am not expressing judgment. As Charles says, It's not the *what* but the *how*. It is just that I have always been my own instrument.

Once in a while I may hold a crystal that I know has been individually attuned to me; but 98 percent of the time, I am my own instrument.

If you want to count Bibles as spiritual tools, then we have five of them in our house. I don't pretend to be a scholar of scripture, but I do enjoy reading from the Bible on a regular basis.

I have never had any interest in the mundane uses of psychic ability, such as seeking to determine the answers to such questions as, "Am I going to date this man?" I've just never cared to use my talents for such stuff.

I've only been interested in the higher angelic levels of light and trying to help people who sincerely really wish to grow spiritually. And even then, my focus is to help people look within—and never to lean on me.

All people have the power of the light within themselves if they will only look.

The Wonderful "Mr. D."

Although the project with Archangel Michael was a major undertaking for me and I feel privileged to have been chosen for the task by such a high-level entity, I will always consider Daephrenocles to be my main source of spiritual guidance.

Charles and I sometimes affectionately call him "Mr. D." By the way, Daephrenocles means, "Healer of Hearts." That is his soul vibration. He stepped aside to allow Archangel Michael to work with me for the purpose of my own spiritual growth, as well as allowing me to do my part to help to bring more light to the planet.

I have learned to identify the manifestations of certain angelic beings by their attendant colors. For instance, a flashing of the colors of yellow and lavender indicates that Daephrenocles is approaching. Archangel Michael flashes blue-violet. The Ascended Master St. Germain appears surrounded by pink-violet. Elijah's color is totally pink. St. John the Beloved is a kind of sea green, while the essence of the disciple Thomas is a lime green. When Thomas appears, he always says, "Prepare, prepare for more service!" Other angelic beings come with a white light.

Not long ago, I saw Daephrenocles hovering above our bed. This is nothing unusual—at least not for me. Most of the time when I see him, it is usually from the waist up. He has a brilliant belt of purple that has something to do with his spiritual power.

I am told that when the time is right, I will see him in full-body. I am told that if I beheld all of him now, it would be overwhelming to me. I've received a tentative promise that maybe I'll get to see him when I'm thirty-eight. I'm thirty-seven now ... still a kid, he says.

A wonderful thing occurred one night in mid-March 1995.

I woke up and looked at Charles. He rolled over and opened his eyes and looked at me. *But I could tell right away that it was not Charles in there!*

He looked at me with a beautiful look of pure love and light. His eyes were just glazed as he looked at me, and he uttered not a word.

I closed my eyes and went back to sleep. I knew *who* it was and what was going on. By soul agreement, Daephrenocles and Charles had changed places for a moment.

You see, Charles and I had had an argument the day before. It was quickly resolved. I can hardly remember what it was about. We don't argue very often. Neither of us enjoys arguing.

Anyway, Daephrenocles was coming in closer to give *both* of us reassurance. And I must say that the experience was reassuring to me and did not bother me in the least.

The next morning, it was Charles waking up with me. I told him about the transfer and why it had occurred. There was no question that the harmony was back between us.

Daephrenocles has often said that *nothing* will be

allowed to come between Charles and me because of the scope of the work that we have to do.

But it *was* Daephrenocles the night before *with* soul permission from Charles, who loves Daephrenocles dearly.

The last time Daephrenocles did anything like that was quite a few years ago when he took my body for a walk from one side of the bed to the other. I remembered nothing. But Charles said that the look in my eyes was different, and I did not behave like me. Daephrenocles said that on the soul level I was off somewhere in a heavenly garden picking flowers.

A Dramatic Dream/Vision Appearance of Archangel Michael

I must share this dream that I had on the morning of March 20, 1995.

I was praying to God to let us know him better and to let us know his angels better. After praying for a while, this dream/vision was given to me:

I was standing in the kitchen of our home. All of a sudden a white mist started to pour forth out of the air and into the kitchen and something started to unfold before me.

At first the mist gave way to many swirling colors.

Within these colors I beheld many sparkling vibrations and frequencies spinning about, as if in a dance.

Then I began to perceive a being of white light. It looked fuzzy to me at first, but then it became more and more clear to my vision.

I know that in this dream I was out of my body and in a different dimension, because it took so much effort to move my arm and my hand.

All of a sudden, the beautiful angel became completely evident to me, hovering before and slightly above me. It represented itself as a male angel dressed in a beautiful flowing white robe.

As he hovered in front of me, he turned his back to me and looked at me over his shoulder. Then he stretched his arm back to me and beckoned me to take his hand.

The beauty of this Angel of Light was indescribable in human words, as it surpassed anything that can be seen upon Earth. I could not begin to do the being justice by trying to provide details of his majesty. He was all white light and appeared without wings.

As I said, I was out-of-the-body, so it took great effort to move my arm and my hand—but I reached up and touched his hand. I remember clearly the tangible feeling of touching the angelic being's hand.

Also, I should mention that I had my eyes open,

something I do not usually do in out-of-body experiences. As soon as the angel took my hand, I heard a very loud whispering voice say these words, *"Look at us!"*

And then I woke up back in my body. I wanted to type an account of the experience right away. I feel very blessed to have had this vision. It had a transformative effect, leaving me with a feeling of peace and calm—as well as gratitude that my prayer had been heard and answered.

I was also told quite clearly that the angel in my dream was Archangel Michael.

I felt like a different person after waking from this dream/vision. I am filled with the knowing that in each moment God is taking care of everything. There is no need to be concerned about how day-to-day needs will be met. It was a very healing and comforting dream.

Honoring Archangel Michael

Over the fireplace mantel in our home, I honor a portrait of Archangel Michael that was painted by our dear friend, the visionary artist Lois East. Lois painted the portrait in 1989, right after Michael first came to me with visions and the expressed desire to bring forth a book of love and inspiration.

The image brought through by Lois is identical to the images that I had been receiving in inner visions from Michael. He had begun appearing in my inner visionary experiences, doing such things as looking upward to heaven and lifting his hands palms upward.

Although I envision Michael with dark hair and a beard, I fully concede that he may appear however he deems necessary to anyone of any race, culture, or language—anywhere on the planet. This is simply how he has come to me, and I have seen his face represented in this fashion many, many times over the years. Indeed, he may appear to another as pure light, or any one of a limitless number of ways. This image is simply the truth that I know as valid within my own soul.

Michael's presence is powerful—and yet so gentle, leading hearts back to the awareness of God.

For others who feel that Michael is attempting to contact them, I urge discernment. Meditate and pray for guidance. There is no limit to how the angelic ones can choose to manifest to those with whom they wish to communicate. Only God knows the reason for each experience, for if the angelic appearance is genuine, its only purpose is to further God's divine plan.

Angels of Light
Received by Lori Jean Flory

We are Angels of Light.

We come in increasing numbers to bring awareness, the vitality of wisdom, the purity of love, the upliftment of truth to your hearts. You are pure light and pure love.

We come to take many hearts home to the eternal light and truth within. It is time for the veils to be lifted and for you to see the beauty that you are.

We are Angels of Light.

We are emissaries of love. We come only to help and we think of nothing for ourselves. We are the purity of the Source, the God Force within the heart.

No once can ever be forced to come to the Light, but we lovingly observe and are there to assist nonetheless.

As you awaken to the grandeur within you, we shall empower you. When you have awakened fully to our presence, we are fully empowered to assist you in your growth.

The more you love, care, share, and assist yourselves and others, the brighter your aura becomes. We are in constant loving observation of this light within you.

It is true that you are clothed in the skin and bone of physicality, but we come to tell you that you are so much more than this. You are light. You are divine. We angelic beings are but a reminder of the radiance that you truly are.

Truly, the teacher appears as the student is ready! Together we are a loving partnership. Many of you are awakening to your true being.

Earth is becoming more light-filled. It is in the process of ascension, and thus, so are her residents. Light is pouring in on Earth as never before. Everyone and everything is experiencing this in their own way. Light is flooding into the sub-atomic levels of the subtle energy bodies as well as the physical body.

Release is occurring on all levels. The DNA of the physical body is becoming re-encoded with more light. The human blueprint is shifting to higher light. Literally, Beloved Ones, you are becoming lighter. There are patterns that are unconscious—not only from this lifetime, but aeons past—that are being released. Many may feel like an onion with the layers being peeled off until the white core of consciousness, the Christ Light, within the heart is remembered.

Many physical, emotional, mental, and spiritual effects are accompanying these dramatic shifts, for it is all Light Body Activation. Many will experience uncertainty and fear, for what was once comfortable, what once worked, no longer is effective. Many are feeling aches within the body. This is not necessarily illness. It is the shift in patterning experienced within the various levels of awareness.

Look for what best serves you in only the highest, most joyous, creative of ways. Look within at the magnificence of your heart.

Many things are changing on all levels. As one grows higher in vibration, certain relationships may fall away. Others may come into your life as new experiences. And some will stay as they were. When there is a difference or shift in vibration, individually and energetically, there may be a difficulty in relating to some. Let them go with your blessings. Many are in different stages of awakening.

*   *   *

Many humans are opening on the Soul level. Veils are removed from their vision as they grow and become more aware of us, the Angels of Light, all around you. You are our reason for being! We are God Force in loving cocreation.

We bless you always!

We are Angels of Light.

The Angels Call Me on the Telephone

On August 21, 1995, I received a brief, but meaningful, message that angelic intelligence tried to leave on our telephone answering machine.

I heard the phone ring. I screen calls sometimes, and just as the machine would have begun to record whomever was on the line, I heard a little voice that sounded kind of electrical say one word, *"Angels,"* and then the machine clicked off.

When I went back to try to see if the voice had been recorded, it sadly had not—but I had received the message! And it was very comforting.

Millions of Angels Are Working with Their Earth Charges

Daephrenocles told me years ago that many master teachers and angels would be working with me, but only the highest and the best would be permitted to pass his watchful guidance.

The angels always seem to be working with me and attuning me. I can feel it when I am resting.

Daephrenocles says that there are millions of angels and master teachers who are working with their Earth charges—and yet most people are not aware of their guides. He is saddened by that—and so pleased that I know of his existence.

Recently, I seem to be perceiving even more Light Beings than ever before, and I'm seeing them with my open eyes. I first see white light, then the outlines of the beings—their heads, necks, robes, and so forth, all filled with white light. I see the sky filled with white sparks of light and pulsating auras. Daephrenocles is always among these beings. I recognize his robe. When I meditate or tune in, I receive the impressions of the words and teachings that they wish to convey.

God knows all of these beings, and they all work for the ONE!

The angels are always there. Millions of them. And they're just waiting for people to become aware of them so that they can work together with all the citizens of Earth for God, the planet, and the blessed oneness that binds the universe together in joyous harmony.